T0064769

The GIFT OF SUCCESS AND HAPPINESS

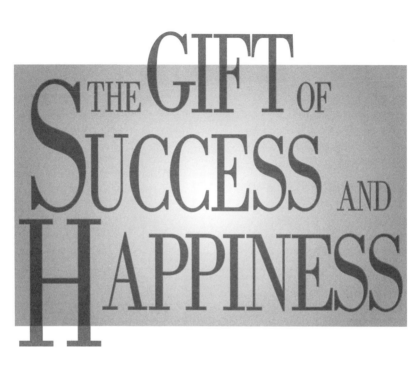

THE GIFT OF SUCCESS AND HAPPINESS

Transforming Your Life Through Business Processing Principles

❖Achieve goals❖Launch a career❖Create a fulfilling social life
❖Save time and money❖Reduce stress❖Maximize happiness

CHIP SAWICKI with VERNON ROBERTS

SKYHORSE PUBLISHING

Skyhorse Publishing books may be purchased in bulk at special discounts for sales promotion, corporate gifts, fund-raising, or educational purposes. Special editions can also be created to specifications. For details, contact the Special Sales Department, Skyhorse Publishing, 307 West 36th Street, 11th Floor, New York, NY 10018 or info@skyhorsepublishing.com.

Skyhorse® and Skyhorse Publishing® are registered trademarks of Skyhorse Publishing, Inc.®, a Delaware corporation.

www.skyhorsepublishing.com

10 9 8 7 6 5 4 3 2 1

Library of Congress Cataloging-in-Publication Data

Sawicki, Chip, 1967-
The gift of success and happiness : transforming your life through business processing principles / Chip Sawicki, with Vernon Roberts.
    p. cm.
ISBN 978-1-61608-280-2 (pbk. : alk. paper)
1. Success. 2. Success in business. 3. Happiness. I. Roberts, Vernon, 1960-
II. Title.
BF637.S8.S29 2011
650.1--dc22
                    2010047308

Printed in China

CONTENTS

PREFACE

This book is authored by Chip Sawicki with Vernon Roberts. The narrative is written in the first person by Chip. He and Vernon worked together and collaborated on every word in the book.

On multiple occasions the authors have been asked these simple yet universally important questions: Are you happy? Are you successful? How do you define happiness and success? Below are the authors' answers to these questions, which will define the basis for the rest of the book.

Chip Sawicki

I have always had a burning curiosity as to how people become successful. When I began my career, I thought that success was only measured in financial terms. Upon achieving financial success, I supposed, one would also achieve happiness.

As my career progressed, jumped forward, stepped back, and then took a few major turns, I had the chance to meet and work with thousands of people from a wide spectrum. I came to know the extremely wealthy and powerful as well as people who had great trouble making ends meet. My personal career started well, and I worked my way up the corporate ladder, receiving raises that put me well above the salary I thought I needed before I started my career. Based on that fact alone, I should have been ecstatic!

Throughout my career my inquisitive nature has allowed me to learn many lessons and to ask probing questions. Not only did I work hard and have fun but I also learned the most from my questioning nature.

As my career matured and my responsibilities increased, I learned that success and happiness are not as codependent as I once thought. Financial success comes from setting and achieving high goals for oneself. Happiness comes from setting reasonable expectations that are achieved on a regular basis. One also needs achievements outside one's career and to give back to the community in order to have a truly fulfilling life.

Vernon Roberts

I worked for twenty years before I began to understand my definition of fulfillment. By that time I'd been married for fourteen years, had four children in a five-year span, and had worked my way to senior vice president, running a corporate learning team. I say I *began* to understand because in that twentieth year I looked back and realized that over the prior three years I'd just begun to discover what success, happiness, and fulfillment looked like for me. The fact was that I wasn't there yet. I'd just let my life happen without a plan but with only a basic idea of where I wanted to go. Because my destination wasn't clear, the path wasn't either. It was like I got on a Greyhound bus and didn't get off for more than a decade because I wasn't sure of my destination. The bus was comfortable and was headed in the direction of someone's definition of success and fulfillment, just not mine. It was a definition that I'd adopted from family and friends while growing up. Many of you can probably understand how that happens. Before I knew what happened, I had a wife, kids, a house, cars, and an MBA. In my heart, though, I really didn't feel successful or fulfilled.

Taking control and mapping out a plan enabled me to fit the more important things that mattered into my life. We all say that a lot of things are important to us, but the truth comes out in where we actually spend our time. In that twentieth year, I left my corporate career and founded my consulting company, Evoke Learning, where I help people move toward their true potential. In 2002, I began a journey that I'm still on eight years later. By creating goals and a structure for my life, I force myself on a daily basis to spend time on the things that are in tune with my goals. Everything you do matters! Life is the journey, so why not enjoy it?

Our Philosophy

In this book we use the principles we learned in the business world to break down the process of life. We make it easy to identify the strengths and weaknesses of our important life decisions. We will show you how, by understanding the process, you gain more and more benefits from it. We start by identifying the three main resources that drive our life: time, finances, and social skills. Then we examine the individual elements of self, career, marriage, home, and children. We then explore the concepts of happiness, financial success, and life achievements in detail. All of these elements comprise what we term "the matrix of life." Upon understanding this matrix of life and the interrelated nature of all of its components, you will be able to use this structure to create your own unique masterpiece.

The Gift of Success and Happiness will benefit people who are preparing to enter the real world, as it will help relieve confusion about the big decisions they are faced with every day and will provide a structure to achieve their goals. The principles in this book will benefit older adults as well, to help them master the challenges of family, career, and finance. This book shows that life is a process that should be taken one step at a time.

The Gift of Success and Happiness will also help bridge the gap between employees and employers. Employees traditionally do not trust their employers, and employers often have difficulty communicating the importance of company initiatives. This book will help employees understand how to maximize their performance at work and minimize their stresses outside of work. Employers will help employees learn that the challenges of managing the finances of the business is very similar to how each person manages their own personal finances . . . only the company has a few more zeroes on the end of their numbers.

This book is also ideal for those who have experienced a few challenging events and are now looking to get back on track with their lives. If you are one of those people, don't despair: everyone makes mistakes in life, and it is not too late to regain a sense of success and happiness. And for those readers who have made poor decisions and now find their lives to be more difficult or challenging than those of their peers, the ideas in this book will help provide structure for your life and help you get back on track toward maximizing your happiness, financial success, and life achievements.

The Gift of Success and Happiness simply illuminates this: There is a process to life. Those who embrace and appreciate it will bear its fruits forever. Those who fight it will be more frustrated and disappointed.

Our wish for you is that you understand the boundaries that exist for all of us and then, within those boundaries, live life by your desires and not those of others. We also hope that you will recognize that your life is up to you and the decisions you make.

This book will challenge you to think of your life in a clearer, structured, and controllable way.

ACKNOWLEDGMENTS

I am sure that all books take a winding path to publication but this one has been touched by many important people, all of them playing an integral role in advancing the concept to reality. My good friend Steve Roberts was essential in getting this process started as we sat in my front yard wondering how we ended up going through significant life-changing events. There were also many, many people who have given me feedback and ideas throughout this process and who are unfortunately too numerous to individually list, but you know that I greatly appreciate all of your help. Then it was Lee Staicer, the best graphic artist I ever met (see Designasaur.com) and good golfing buddy, who helped me take my initial manuscript and transform it into a book. Another good friend, Steve van Niman, helped me develop the website and print and distribute my initial draft version. At this point I met Vernon Roberts—the best professional speaker I have ever witnessed. He liked the book and the concepts but it wasn't until we were able to get the book published that we could formally offer the seminar that will help many people maximize their success and happiness.

Originally, my working title for this book was *Achieve Your American Dream*, which was a bit ironic as I obtained my biggest break while in South Africa. That is where I met Greg Euson. He was the one who introduced me to my agent, Herb Schaffner. I had a general disdain for agents from my professional sports days but Herb proved how valuable agents are in this industry. He took my manuscript and helped Vernon and me turn it into a real book! Without his guidance, network, and wealth of knowledge of the tricks of the trade, there is no way I could have made it to this point.

I am also extremely grateful for the folks at Skyhorse Publishing. Specifically, it was Julie Matysik and Bill Wolfsthal who saw the potential and took a chance on us. I hope that every author can have the privilege of working with such a professional, creative, and entrepreneurial publisher.

It is also very important for me to recognize the real strength of family, who have supported me not only through this process but also in all aspects of my life. In addition to being my parents, Priscilla and Chuck have also been great mentors and friends. I would also like to acknowledge my sons, Zach and Trent, for teaching me patience and how fulfilling life can be with two great children. Then there is the most important person in my life, my wife Lisa. Without her support and encouragement, I could have never made it through this process.

And finally, I would like to thank those of you who bought this book and helped to make it a success. Because of you, my wife has been forced to utter the three sweetest words a husband can hear, "You were right!"

—Chip Sawacki

Many thanks are due to Chip Sawicki for inviting me to collaborate with him on this book. Ever since we met at a Toastmasters meeting three years ago, he has been single minded in his quest to bring this book to all of you. I have been writing articles for my client newsletters, blog, and website for the past five years and this book has allowed me to share concepts about accountability and life management for which I have much passion.

Thanks also go to for four special people in my life. My parents, Vernon Sr. and Muriel, who have provided encouragement and support since I was a child, and are always there for my family. To Lynn Carnes, my mentor and friend of fourteen years, for believing in me at Bank of America in the spring of 1997 and allowing me to find and pursue my passion for teaching and my deep spirituality. HUGE thanks go to my wife Nancy, who has her own successful management career. Nancy has been supportive of my entrepreneurial spirit. She has provided love, help, and encouragement on a daily basis for the past twenty-two years.

—Vernon Roberts

CHAPTER 1:
INTRODUCTION

The ultimate example of the person who has The Gift is Bill Gates, cofounder of Microsoft. Gates possesses this gift not because of his tremendous wealth but because of the order in which he has decided to live his life. First, he dedicated himself to starting Microsoft. Then, upon finding more time in his hectic schedule, he became a successful husband and father. After that, he found more time by turning over the reins as Microsoft's CEO to Steve Ballmer. This enabled him to head down the path toward fully realizing The Gift as he and his wife, Melinda, steadily increase the amount of time and focus they are able to give to their life passion: the Bill & Melinda Gates Foundation, which is the world's largest charitable foundation.

Tom Hicks was a businessman who founded a very successful leveraged buyout firm, enabling him to fulfill one of his life dreams when he purchased the Texas Rangers. After this, he abandoned The Gift by putting the team into too much debt and heightening the player payroll too much. As a result, he was forced to sell the team.

Desiree DeStefano was at the peak of her career as a top executive at a Fortune 1000 company, but she felt her life was lacking; she ultimately wanted children. Realizing The Gift enabled her to resign from her demanding position and pursue a career that required less of her time so that she could have the balance that she needed in her life.

As for myself, I was in the midst of a very successful career and a great family situation when, all of a sudden, my world turned upside down when I left my executive position at the Texas Rangers and Dallas Stars organization. In another twist, my wife decided to pursue a fantastic opportunity in her career that required us to relocate. It was at this point that life forced me to discover The Gift.

Here is The Gift: Whatever we believe spiritually or politically, whatever our talents and career goals may be, we can only achieve happiness and success by changing *how* we do things. By understanding the simple but elusive *process* that eliminates stress and distraction, we give our lives a *structure* that supports our work, family, and faith.

The Gift is the hidden structure that supports all success and happiness.

Basic mind theory tells us that our brain has two parts. At its simplest level, without discussing a lot of theory, our brain has an emotional side and a logical side. These two sides are a part of every human being and help to make us who we are. Each of us uses a mixture of emotion and logic to deal with all facets of our lives. The logical part tells us how we go about doing something; the emotional part guides how we handle it. You experience this on a daily basis in your home and work life. One example is when you receive feedback from someone you dislike. Your logical side knows that you need to listen to the feedback while your emotional side is fuming, hurt, and wants to either retaliate or walk away. While you're reading this book, it will be important to keenly observe your emotional side and isolate those detrimental thoughts. It's true that we all experience emotions and that this is a part of what makes us human. However, we are asking you to observe objectively your actions as if they were in a glass box on the table in front of you. As you read more, our directive will become clearer.

When Vernon and I were sitting over coffee in one of our many discussions about emotion and logic, he told me this story: Many years ago, he was shopping for a car at one of the national "one price" pre-owned mega retailers. Prior to going, he had done the math and knew what he was looking for and the amount he could afford. After driving what was in his price range, he unexpectedly noticed a German luxury car. Knowing human nature, the salesperson said, "Don't test drive it if it's out of your price range." Despite this warning, Vernon drove the luxury car, adjusted his calculations, and purchased the car. What happened here? We'll just call it emotional override. He let his emotions come before his logical and realistic budget calculations. This is why we ask that you closely observe your emotional side as you work through this book. That's a crucial part of The Gift.

Perhaps you will discover The Gift when you graduate from college and take that important first step in starting your career or deciding to pursue additional education. For others, it may be a first career change, a divorce and remarriage, a painful journey of self-discovery, or learning how to be an effective parent. At some point in life, each of us will throw the gates open and see ahead of us the goals we seek. The real key to success and happiness is learning how to stay in the race for the rest of our lives and win on our individual terms. During the race, you will encounter new freedoms, responsibilities, excitements, stresses, opportunities, and fears. The Gift is the structure that will enable you to balance it all.

A proper education lays the foundation to increase your chances for success and happiness but by no means does it guarantee it. The lack of a traditional education does not prevent success and happiness, but you will need to do some serious learning through other means. It is clear to me that when you stop learning, you stop growing and achieving. We live in a dynamic world, and if you don't keep pace, you will be left behind.

In this book, you will begin on the path of knowledge and decision making that leads to The Gift. This path has taken me over two decades to travel. Along the way, I have met thousands of people from all different areas and spent endless hours understanding that success and happiness may look different for each individual, but the path traveled is surprisingly similar. Consistently, I found that each successful individual continuously improved their "personal process," which helped them succeed in all aspects of life.

Whatever our calling, talents, wealth, or accomplishments, we will not finish the race if we do not manage stress and understand the requirements of living well in a complex society. Through this book, you will learn how to follow the path that is common to successful and happy people but has managed to elude and frustrate far too many of us in our society.

The first life lesson we teach will lay the foundation for the rest of this book. Lesson number one is that you must develop the ability and awareness to learn from other people's mistakes. If you can do this, you will save a great amount of time, money, and embarrassment throughout your life. The start of this process, for me, was to learn from the many mistakes I have made over the last two decades. Many of those mistakes seem quite comical now, but I assure you that they were not at the time they happened. In the coming chapters, I will share my mistakes and (thankfully) my many successes. If you take lesson one to heart, my experiences will provide you with some data to chart a path to accentuate your strengths and maximize your chances of success and happiness.

Success in life is not based on the wealth of the family you were born into but rather on the quality of the advice and guidance you are given throughout your life. This book will:

1. Provide the structure that supports success and happiness.
2. Offer detailed guidance and advice for success in each core element of your life.
3. Help you avoid unnecessary stress that plagues unhappy people.
4. Aid you in facilitating good decisions.

The Matrix of Life

What do we mean by the matrix of life? A matrix is an arrangement of materials or parts that illustrates how those parts are interconnected. In biology, a matrix is the substance that grows between cells to form our bodies. We demonstrate here that the elements of our lives can best be managed by viewing them as a matrix. You cannot change one element in a matrix without affecting another. These elements are interconnected and grow or change in our relationship to one another. If one element is failing, it affects the others. Conversely, if one element is healthy, it strengthens the others.

The following is a graphical depiction of how stress, the core elements of life, happiness, financial success, and achievements are interrelated. This book will address each factor separately and then provide you with a structure to build your personal matrix.

This matrix is seen through the core elements of life below that we all recognize:

- Self
- Career
- Marriage/Relationship
- Home
- Children

Each core element will be addressed in detail so you can understand the common characteristics of success and failure in each. Only two core elements are mandatory: self and career. You must take care of yourself and you must be able to afford your chosen lifestyle. As for the other elements, not everyone *needs* to get married or have a committed relationship; not everyone *needs* to buy a home; and not everyone *needs* to have children. However, if you decide to commit to a relationship, buy a home, or have children, you *must* have the desire, time, and money needed for making these commitments successful. Self and career are the essential core elements that lay a solid foundation for the rest of your life. Then as each core element is mastered, you will have the time and money available to add the next core element to your life. The chaos created by adding an element before you are ready will seriously impair your future success and happiness.

The Three Drivers

When building your life, it is important to understand that three main drivers have a strong influence over our emotional lives. When managed effectively, these drivers are valuable resources. When overcommitted, they cause a level of stress that can impair happiness. The three drivers focus on how we use our time, how we handle our finances, and how we see ourselves integrating into society. We call these **time**, **financial**, and **social** drivers. As in a typical matrix, each driver has a relationship to the other two. Each can strengthen or weaken the others. In this book, we'll discuss these drivers from the perspective of how they create stresses in our lives that inhibit our happiness. If you've ever felt stressed, you can bet that it comes from one of these three stresses. Let's take a look at each of them.

Time Stress—everyone is allocated the exact same amount of time each week, 168 hours. What makes each of us different is how we utilize that time. This book will help you understand how to budget and maximize your time (just as you should manage your money).

Financial Stress—there are two aspects to financial stress: earnings and expenses. This book will help you understand your earnings potential and how to best fulfill that potential. It will also help you set a budget for expenses based on your current income. If your expenses exceed your income, you are guaranteed to have financial stress. Money may not make you happy, but not managing it properly *will* make you miserable. The good news is that there are easy methods to employ in order to establish your expectations and to better manage your personal budget so that you will be able to avoid financial stress.

Social Stress—Social stress results from how you see yourself fitting in. Are you trying to be more (or less) than who you are? It is important for you to understand your strengths and weaknesses. You need to work consistently on improving your weaknesses, accentuating your positives, and not concerning yourself with what you cannot change. Social groups are based on a variety of different factors, such as common interests, age, gender, career path, where you live, or even athletic ability. It is important that you find positive social groups in which you feel comfortable. If you try to force yourself to fit in with a group of people with whom you have little in common, you will feel uncomfortable and your social stress will be high.

Correlating Happiness and Success

Happiness is one of the most interesting words in the English language. We all know exactly what it is, but when asked for a definition, we would all most certainly define it differently. Why is this? The reasoning is that happiness depends on what you are thinking of at the time you are asked for a definition—in that way, it is fluid. Are you thinking about traveling, a relationship, your job, your friends, a game, school commitments, children, or where you live?

Your level of happiness is the strongest indicator of whether the vital elements of your life are in a healthy, vibrant balance. We will examine what makes you happy and your current level of happiness for each of the core elements of your life. As you assess your happiness as determined by each element, you will better understand what areas of your life are functioning properly and which areas need improvement.

Financial success is a contributing factor in overall contentment because it will help you afford a lifestyle that brings you the maximum amount of happiness. Each core element you add to your life—such as a relationship, house, or children—has the same thing in common; they all cost more money! Keep in mind that achieving financial success does not guarantee that you will be happy, though.

As you add more of the five core elements to your life, your definition of success will change and expand to include your life achievements. The traditional measures to gauge financial success in your career, however, are not applicable to measuring success in the other core elements of your life.

Now let me share a surprising observation I made while writing this book: Happiness and success actually have a lower-than-expected correlation. Many people associate money with happiness, so you may find the low correlation somewhat surprising. In reality, happiness is achieved by setting reasonable *expectations*. Expectations are generally static and are met on a regular, almost daily, basis. Success is reached by setting and accomplishing *goals*. Goals change throughout your life and are not accomplished as often as expectations are met. Upon accomplishing one set of goals, you set new, higher goals to strive for toward the next level of success. All too often, people who set high goals also set high expectations, and when they are unable to meet those high expectations they become chronically dissatisfied with their performance and life situation. Conversely, some people set very low goals and expectations and, due to this, fail to achieve a desired level of success. Since their expectations are so low, these people are sometimes perfectly content.

This balance of happiness and success can cause a dilemma for any person. You must decide how much time you want to sacrifice in order to achieve future success. If you decide not to sacrifice much time, you must set your expectations for happiness at a level that correlates to the amount of time you have dedicated; it is that simple. On the flip side, if someone dedicates too much of his or her time to success for an extended period of time, it is likely he or she will not be happy. This book aims to help you understand the natural balance between happiness and success.

Creating Your Own Matrix and Making Changes

Once you understand the benefits and sacrifices of each core element of life, you will then be able to view your own matrix and make any appropriate changes.

During school it is obviously important to score good grades because students are evaluated and ranked by those grades. While it is not a foolproof process, good grades generally represent not only intelligence but also point to an individual who has developed the best personal habits possible (i.e., organization, decision making, positive attitude, and personal responsibility). Considering those grades, along with an interview to assess interpersonal skills, is the most effective way for an employer to make the best hiring decision possible in order to fill their company's needs.

Once hired, you need to develop a new set of skills to be successful (i.e., industry expertise, teamwork, customer service, management skills, and administrative skills). Those who adapt the fastest in this arena excel the most.

If you enter into a time-consuming relationship or have children too early, what happens to your level of career or financial success? You do not have the time to develop those new skills. Your peer group will have a distinct competitive advantage: namely, time. This is why you *must* master the first level before you can advance and be fully prepared for the next step.

The simplest matrix of life is to go to school, get a good job, stay single, rent an apartment or house, and travel freely. The most fulfilling matrix, however, is typically also the most complex because it includes experiencing *all* of the core elements in tandem. Achieving the full matrix is much easier if you commit to each core element in the order recommended in this book, because each element lays a solid foundation for the next. If you have made some unwise decisions—and have a desire to live a better life—the principles in this book will be a critical aspect of your course correction.

Remember, you can do anything you want in life, but you can't do *everything* at the same time. Throughout this book are worksheets that will help you build your personal matrix and develop a plan to ensure that you have proper structure in your daily life. Proper structure will ultimately lead you to making good decisions. In turn, good decisions will allow you to live the fullest life possible.

CHAPTER 2:
SO YOU HAD SOME CHALLENGES . . .
WHO HASN'T?

Irish writer Oliver Goldsmith once said, "Success consists of getting up just one more time than you fall." Many may hide the mistakes they make better than others but, in the end, we all are at fault and experience challenges. In fact, mistakes are actually important to our personal development. Mistakes let us know where our boundaries are. The right kind of mistake consistently pushes and expands the boundaries that help us develop and mature.

So have you had some recent challenges, either at work, at school, or in your personal life? Sure you have . . . and you will surely have more throughout your life. As we have stated before, this book focuses on giving you a clearly defined structure for your life so that you can make the best decisions possible based upon your passions, strengths, and desires. A significant part of life is having challenges and learning from them (although it is better to learn from others' challenges whenever possible). Some people just happen to experience more dramatic challenges than others. Your personal challenges can certainly inhibit your potential for happiness, financial success, and achievements but they do not mean that you must endure being miserable.

The information in this chapter will help you understand common traits that successful people possess when dealing with common challenges. It will also address situations that can prevent people from overcoming challenges, allowing them to permanently impair their future potential for happiness and success.

Today Is the First Day of the Rest of Your Life

Effective immediately, you must forgive yourself for whatever mistakes you have made in the past. You must also forgive anyone whose mistakes have personally affected you. There is nothing you can do to change your past, and you are the only one who can make the future better. It is time to accept responsibility and start getting your life back on track. Change what you can change and accept the rest as experience.

Before you advance too far into this book, I must confess that I may come across as rather neurotic due to the various "structures" I propose that you follow for a successful and fulfilled life. As a result, it is possible that you will want to ask of me: "Do you personally use all of the worksheets that you have included throughout this book?" The answer, of course, is no (note that I *am* fanatical about keeping my calendar, an accurate checkbook, and a list of "to-dos"). The worksheets included in this book were created to help demonstrate the points made within the pages of the book. You may find that you do not need to fill out each sheet, but they are provided as tools to help you plan for, and achieve, the maximum level of success and happiness you are able in life.

It is true that no one will use 100 percent of the worksheets for the rest of his or her life. The better you get at thinking in a structured way, the less you will rely on the worksheets in this book. Most successful people think in a highly structured way. By properly using the worksheets, you will dramatically increase your level of effectiveness in structuring your life. Thus, you will have the opportunity to learn in only a few hours what took me two decades to master.

Why Do Bad Things Happen to Me?

It is important to understand why bad things happen. Bad things happen primarily due to bad decisions resulting from inadequate structure in your life. Proper structure (i.e., setting goals, identifying expectations, budgeting money, and managing time effectively) will force good decisions because each decision will then have relevance. When you have clearly defined and achievable goals, you can ask yourself, "Does this decision get me closer to my goals?" This will give each decision the relevance that may not have previously existed. There are two other main reasons why people make bad decisions. The first is boredom. You must keep yourself occupied with productive and positive activities (i.e., a job, additional education, home projects, or volunteer work) so that you do not become bored. Boredom causes many good people to make bad decisions. The second reason for making bad decisions stems from any involvement in a negative social circle. You are influenced and judged by the company you keep. You must be sure that your social circle has a positive effect on the decisions you make and the way you are perceived. If you are involved in a negative social circle, this can be one of the most difficult changes to make in your life—but it is absolutely essential that you make it.

Do You Want to Fix Your Problems?

Many people have problems that they do not fix for a variety of reasons. The main reasons are as follows:

- They like the sympathy and attention they get from other people.
- They do not want to make changes (particularly to social circles).
- They do not want to work hard.
- They are overwhelmed and don't know where to start (meaning, they don't have proper structure).

The only valid reason is the last one. It is not coincidence or "luck" that people become successful. They became that way because they worked hard and had a structured approach to their life that gave them a framework for forcing good decisions. If you do not have the proper structure in your life naturally, then you should use the worksheets in this book until the process becomes routine.

You can fix your problems, but it usually requires hard work and sacrifice. You should first focus on what you can change and control easily before tackling the more challenging problems.

Compartmentalize Your Problems

Sometimes when people are having trouble in one area of their lives, they allow it to affect all the areas of their lives. A bad relationship, a difficult situation at work, problems with your house, and poorly behaved children are all examples of problems that can create stress. The best way to handle these situations is to identify which part of your life is being affected by using the Time Allocation and the Personal Budget worksheets. Then, identify how you are going to obtain the necessary time and money, change your behavior, or reset your goals and expectations to solve the problem. When you see it on paper, you will be surprised at how easy it is to shift your resources to adequately address your problems. The worksheets we have included are important tools to help you implement proper structure in your life. Once you have done this you will realize that you have control over the situation.

A few notes of caution:

- Be careful not to let personal issues affect other areas of your life. Personal issues are generally emotional in nature. These issues can cause an infinite time drain if you allow them to. Compartmentalize these issues so that they can be controlled in a small area of your life. Be sure to dedicate enough time and energy to the other important areas, particularly your child(ren) and career, to ensure those areas do not suffer any consequences.
- Divorce is not necessarily the fix you think it is. Everyone has problems at certain points in their marriage. You should communicate the problems in a clear, rational way (in writing is one good option) and do everything you can to work through these problems. Be open to the fact that you may be causing some of the issues you are experiencing as a couple—relationship problems are rarely isolated to one person. Ensure that there are

permanent, irreconcilable problems that cannot be resolved before you resort to divorce. Remember, if you have children, you will have a relationship with your spouse—even if you are divorced—for the rest of your life, whether you like it or not.

* Do not make any rash decisions when it comes to your job. Identify where the problem lies. Is it temporary, permanent, or do you not have the right expectations? The best way to get perspective is to interview for a new job while you still have your current job.
* Compartmentalize your problem(s) so that it does not cause all areas of your life to spiral out of control.

Set New Expectations and Goals to Make Sure They Are Achievable

Take some time and be honest with yourself. How much have your challenges inhibited your potential happiness, financial success, and achievements? Once you have answered this, use the worksheets toward the end of this book to help you reset your expectations and goals. This will be an important step toward again gaining control over your life. It must work on paper before it works in reality. If you have a sense of control over the things that happen in your life, you are guaranteed to be much happier and more successful overall.

Clear the Clutter

Once you have adequately prioritized your life, you can clear away all of the nonessential commitments on your resources (like friends and family who drain your time and patience for no productive reason). This process of getting back to the basics will help you see what is truly important in life. This process is not necessarily easy and will likely require a combination of the following:

* Short-term sacrifice of happiness
* Cut spending on anything that is nonessential
* Reduction of time spent with friends
* Elimination of time spent helping others with their problems

- Less time watching television
- Possible downsizing of where you live or what you drive
- Increased support for a spouse who is the revenue generator
- Less socializing at work

Create a plan so that you understand the sacrifices required to ensure that you emerge stronger and more successful from this difficult time in your life.

Ask for Help

This directive seems so simple, and you might be wondering why I am wasting time and space writing about it. However, I have found that too many people do not ask for help. Perhaps some are too proud to ask for help, or some just don't know how to do it properly. Your family will always be the best and easiest group to look to for help. Always remember that people generally like to help one another but they hate being told what to do. Also, as soon as you ask for help, you must be ready to make certain compromises. For example:

- If you move into someone's home, he is afforded the rights to make the rules.
- Always show your appreciation for anyone who gives you help—help is not something to be expected.
- Help those who help you in any way you can.
- Listen to the advice that comes along with the help—it may prove worthwhile.

It's possible that you may find yourself asking for help with money in the near (or far) future. Just remember that when someone does loan you money, be openly gracious about the loan and work your hardest to pay the person back in a timely fashion. This way, if you ever need to borrow money again, you will not have burned any bridges and will be more likely to receive help again.

When you are trying to get out of debt, make sure you actively work to change all the behaviors that led you to getting into debt in the first place. If you do not change those bad habits, you *will* find yourself in debt again. If you ask for money to help pay your debts but do not also change your spending patterns, do not expect help from that same person again. He will notice that giving you money is clearly only a temporary fix for your problem (I call this using a garden hose on a forest fire). Consequently, he will be wasting money if he relinquishes more to you in the future.

There are also many not-for-profit organizations and government agencies that can help you with financial problems. Some simple research through the Internet or at your local library can go a long way to setting you on the path toward reducing debt and starting fresh.

You May Need to Leave Your Comfort Zone

Solving your problems often requires placing yourself in a new situation or social group (i.e., obtaining a new job, relocating, removing negative influences, or exiting a bad relationship). Many people do not want to make these difficult changes, and so they remain in a rut for life. To solve certain problems, you *must* be able to leave your comfort zone, especially if you find that elements within that zone have a clearly negative effect on your everyday life. This is also why it is important to avoid negative social groups from the very beginning, whether at college, in the workplace, in your relationships with others, or even in your neighborhood. Once you are involved with a negative peer group, it can become very difficult to divorce yourself from the situation.

Reward Yourself

Change can certainly be difficult; however, don't allow change to become overwhelming. Break it down into components. Set up milestones to further break down each of these components into manageable steps. Upon completing a milestone, it is important to set up a system of rewards so that you can celebrate the progress you are making. Some of the best rewards to use are the simple things that you enjoy, such as a meal at a favorite restaurant or tickets to a sporting event.

Return to School

Many bad decisions occur when we are rather young. It is common for young people to stop their education during this period of time. A great way to get back on track is to return to school. This is important for several reasons:

* You will catch up to the qualifications of your peers.
* You will find new peer groups that may have a more positive effect on you.
* It is a safe environment in which to "recreate" yourself.

Sometimes returning to school is not an option. In this case, taking an apprenticeship to learn a skilled trade is a good alternative. Another option is to enlist in the military. You will certainly learn good habits and self-discipline, and surround yourself with positive, like-minded people. You will also be a part of an organization in which you can feel tremendous pride. There is no more noble effort than protecting this country's freedom and interests. Furthermore, you will have the ability to receive money for college when your tour of duty is completed, if you choose to leave the military and continue to pursue your education.

Don't Lose Your Sense of Humor

Difficult things happen to us—and to those around us—throughout our lives. Sometimes these trying situations can bring on depression, anxiety, and generally put you in a rut that is difficult to emerge from. However, if you are able to look at the situation objectively and try to insert a little bit of humor into it, you will have a much better time coping with the difficulties that lie ahead. Don't let the negative situation affect your ability to laugh things off. Humor will always help you find the bright light at the end of the tunnel— no matter how long or dark that tunnel may be.

Never Underestimate the Value of Hard Work

Hard work is usually the first—and most crucial—step toward getting back on track. If you've had more challenges in your life as compared to your peers, this means that you will need to prepare yourself to work even harder to catch up (and to not fall further behind). A common factor that can cause challenging situations in the first place is the *lack* of hard work.

Hard work enables you to have a fulfilling life.

Don't Double Down

Your first mistake rarely gets you into irreversible trouble. Many people try to quickly catch up for the mistakes they have made, particularly ones that have affected their financial success. I call this the "doubling down" effect. People take larger and larger risks to try to catch up. Yet all this does is put these people into deeper and deeper financial trouble. This is why gambling without money you can afford to lose is so dangerous—and is a real problem in our society.

Stop negative cycles as soon as possible. Start a positive cycle today by making one good decision at a time.

Are You a Complainer?

Not born with a silver spoon in your mouth? Don't worry; it does not help as much as you think. People who have had more challenges growing up are generally more experienced and motivated than those who lead a so-called "easy" life. Up until your mid twenties, the "silver spooners" generally do have it easier. But at about age twenty-five, their paths cross with the rest of society and it becomes all about what you have done for yourself, not what your parents have done for you.

Yes, life can certainly be unfair, and some people will constantly complain about the bad hand they have been dealt. These people spend so much time and effort complaining that they have no time left to do anything productive. These people can also be a drain on your time as well. This sounds negative, but some people simply cannot be helped (until they want to be). Do not become this person, and be stern in removing these people from your life. A little less complaining and a little more action will help you more than just about anything else.

Are You a Contrarian?

Would you rather be right more than 90 percent of the time or less than 10 percent? Some people live for that rare occasion when they are correct and the masses are wrong. Although this event can be extremely rewarding, it comes with tremendous frustration during the other 90 percent of his or her life.

That being said, it is also important not to blindly follow the masses. It is a delicate balance to go with the flow and still think independently. The most successful people are "strategic contrarians."

PART I

PRIMARY SOURCES OF STRESS

The first section of this book defines the three main drivers that provide the valuable resources and stressful constraints for the foundation of life. They are as follows:

- Time stress
- Financial stress
- Social stress

Time, money, and social capabilities are all resources that allow us to build the foundation of our lives. I use the term "stress" to indicate when each of these capabilities is in some way limited and stress results from the challenge of making effective use of each. There is a proper level of stress, which occurs when you maximize how you leverage these valuable resources. This is why people are usually most productive when they have less time to complete a task. When the limits of these resources are stretched too far, the stress becomes unmanageable. For example, people will be overly stressed if they do not have enough money to pay their bills.

The following three chapters address each of these three drivers that, when overcommitted, produce the most stress in our lives. Once we understand the resources and constraints that form the foundation of our lives and how to manage the resulting stress, we will then move on to understanding the core elements of life.

CHAPTER 3:
TIME STRESS

Each of us is equal in many ways—we are equal in the eyes of our Creator, in our inalienable rights as humans, and as citizens in the United States. We are also equal in another way: each of us has only 168 hours per week. What we do with those 168 hours, however, makes each of us different. You must learn to manage your time the same way you manage your money, and this chapter will provide you with the tools to budget your time and to maximize those precious 168 hours each week.

When Vernon and I conduct workshops, Vernon refers to these weekly hours as the "Power of 168." At a workshop, Vernon will ask his audience to imagine each hour as a precious jewel that must be managed and accounted for. He also shares the story of how, one day while visiting Amsterdam, he found himself gazing at a huge painting on a museum wall. *Battle of Waterloo* by Jan Willem Pieneman was an astounding 18 feet high and 27 feet wide and captivated his curiosity, so he walked up to it, stopping only a few feet away. Standing so close, Vernon could not take in the whole canvas, so he slowly backed up. As he did so, the painting took form and the whole picture began to come together. Impressed that artist could create such a beautiful and large piece of art, Vernon did a web search and discovered that a painting of that size could be successfully made by starting with a sketch and then drawing a grid on to the canvas and painting in each square of the grid.

Vernon talks about two distinct lessons from this encounter. The first lesson was about perspective. Sometimes, you need to step back and assess the entire "picture" in order to make sense of all its components. Just like viewing the painting from an adequate distance, we need to learn to step back and attain perspective on all the events in our lives. Each event may have an effect on some other element in our matrix of life; nothing happens in a vacuum. Think back to our earlier example about Vernon and the German car he bought on an emotional impulse. If Vernon had just stepped back a little, he may have made a different (and better) choice. When in doubt or if you feel that you are being pushed into a situation, always step back and take time to take in the full picture and weigh all of your options.

The second lesson is about structure. The process of creating grids to break down an overwhelming task will make it easier to complete. When we reference the Power of 168, we're asking you to visualize 168 grids that you populate with activities during the week, which create the life you are living (1 grid = 1 hour per week).

The Core Elements of Life

When you budget your time, you must categorize your time requirements by the core elements of life: self, career, marriage/ relationship, home, and (if so) children. This makes it easy to determine where you are speeding the most of your time. How many "grids" are you allocating for the important elements of your life? We have heard many people talk about what is important to them, only to uncover that they never placed these core elements into their matrix. A mentor once told me that a person would have difficulty being successful if he possessed high standards but no work ethic. I know you have probably encountered one of these people through the years: they tend to be all talk and no action. They see the goal in the distance but complain about the journey they must take in order to get there. The bottom line is that each of these elements requires your time or they will become problematic for you. The two core elements of life that are absolutely mandatory for you to master are self and career.

Self is the category of time that is required to take care of your personal needs (i.e., sleep, eating, education, fun). *Career* demands time to enable you to afford the lifestyle you wish to maintain. There may come a day when you choose not to have a career, but this will most likely be because you are married to a partner whose earnings allow you to afford your lifestyle on one income. The optional categories include marriage/relationships, home, and children.

All three of these optional categories require additional time on your part to ensure their success. If you are unsure about how or why you will dedicate the time these important commitments require, you must examine your goals and your priorities. Do not get married and have children if you have doubts about making such a time commitment; without the investment of your time, your marriage will fail, or you will find yourself frustrated as a parent.

If you overcommit to various tasks or hypothesize that you can handle all of these priorities by cutting into your sleep or leaving less than adequate time for yourself, you can be sure you will soon experience a negative level of stress.

Keep this in mind: Our lives in the 2000s take place in a much more demanding world in terms of time and organization than previous generations experienced. Time stress has increased dramatically because technology has made it possible to pursue an increased number of communication and leisure options. Due to technological advancements, you are now reachable twenty-four hours a day, seven days a week. In the past, it was much easier for a person to "disappear" for periods of time, enabling him to recharge his batteries. Now, although it allows for more flexibility in many areas, technology has also contributed to less downtime and can also cause people to be less "fresh" when handling difficult situations, simply because they are overstimulated throughout the day. If one thing is for certain, never underestimate the importance of being "fresh." The ability to make decisions and respond to others in a clear and effective manner is severely hampered if you are functioning at less than 100 percent. If this is the case, no communication would be better than poor communication, so keep that in mind.

Today, citizens in America and other modern democracies have greater access to information, entertainment, and travel. If compared to the same options available even up until the mid-twentieth century, our opportunities to visit destinations all over the globe, to communicate via the computer and smartphones, and to spend our leisure time have shifted radically. In short, we have many more options today in the above categories than we did in the past—and we will continue to have more as we move in to the future.

Most of us can see the positives of those options but often underestimate the negatives, particularly the reality that they all use part of our precious 168 hours per week. Travel, nightlife, socializing with friends, trips to Vegas, skiing, or whatever it may be—these activities require time. If time is used for these activities, it is not available for other necessary tasks. Remember that you must be sure to dedicate the time necessary to properly take care of your basic needs, such as sleeping and eating properly. You also need to make sure that you are dedicating the appropriate amount of time to your career to ensure that you can afford your chosen lifestyle.

Time Allocation Worksheet

Just as you *must* manage your money, you must also manage your time. To facilitate this process, I have developed a worksheet for time allocation, displayed on page 38 (also available in a more user-friendly, printable version at TheSuccessGift.com). By using this worksheet, you will learn discipline and time-management skills. You will also be able to control how and where you spend your 168 hours (336 hours for those who are married). The worksheet provides the opportunity for you to perform "what if" scenarios as you prepare to include the optional core elements in your life. As you go through this exercise, you will discover the following:

- 168 hours is not as much time as you thought it was.
- The more core elements of life you open, the more time-constrained you will be.
- Life is complicated because we have so many more options to manage and choices to make than our parents had, and only the same amount of time in which to accomplish these options.

This tool will empower you to avoid time stress in a very proactive way. The key is *not* to make a time commitment unless you have the adequate amount of minutes, hours, or days to complete it. Once you have agreed to something, you have no choice but to fulfill your commitment—and this can lead to unnecessary time stress if not planned out properly.

Remember: If your use of time does not work on paper, it certainly won't work in reality!

Time Allocation Worksheet

Self:
- Activities
- Breakfast
- Church
- Dinner
- Errands
- Exercise
- Hobbies
- Homework
- Laundry
- Lunch
- Paying bills
- Read
- School
- Shopping
- Shower/dressed
- Sleep
- Socializing
- Sports
- Volunteering
- Watch television
- Other:

Total | 0

Career:
- Career Advancement
- Commute
- Continuing Ed.
- Functions
- Networking
- Travel
- Work hours
- Other:

Total | 0

Significant Other:
- Time together
- Going out
- "Honey-Do's"
- Other:

Total | 0

Home:
- Clean house
- Clean pool
- Make repairs
- Mow lawn
- Remodeling
- Other:

Total | 0

Children:
- Activities
- Feeding
- Getting ready
- Homework
- Monitoring
- Sports
- Volunteering
- Other:

Total | 0

Pets:
- Walking
- Feeding
- Training
- Attention
- Other:

Total | 0

	SINGLE	MARRIED
Total hours available	168	336
Total hours allocated	0	0

Comfortable/(Stressed)

Getting Married Means You Have 336 Hours

One of the many challenges of marriage or relationships is balancing priorities and responsibilities. This will be covered further in chapter 8 but there is a quick point that needs to be highlighted now. Each partner must acknowledge who is the provider, who is the caretaker, or if these roles are shared equally. Assuming these roles are not shared equally, the caretaker needs to do as much as possible to free up the time of the provider so that the provider can focus on achieving the level in his or her career that will generate the couple's desired income level. The key in any relationship, in regards to time, is to minimize duplication of effort.

Collaborate, don't compete. This is one of the hardest lessons I've learned in life. When we were first married, my wife and I felt like we had to do everything together, even the basic tasks like grocery shopping. We felt that when we weren't working, we were supposed to be together because that was the ingrained impression of marriage we both held. This was not a significant problem until we had children . . . then *boom!* Our world was turned upside down. There was simply not enough time to get everything done together. At that point, we were forced to realize that we had to adapt. Once we started to divide and conquer life's basic tasks, we discovered we were twice as efficient and our stress levels subsided.

Order Is Important

We are exposed to so many different opportunities now based on what we view and learn on TV and the Internet. In this day and age you can do anything you want, but you can't do everything. In this book, a consistent theme is this: *Order is important.* While going through the process of writing this book, I have discovered that you will have a much higher chance of adding depth to your life if you realize that you must take life one step at a time. You need to open one core element of life at a time and you should do it in a reasonable order. If you are taking care of your personal needs, you will be more effective in other areas. Upon establishing a solid career, you will be able to dedicate the necessary time to have a positive relationship. The benefits of a solid career and a positive, established relationship will make taking care of your house, and (if any) children, much easier. If you go out of order, you will likely feel long-term stress and, at the very least, frustration for not achieving as many of your goals and expectations as your peers.

Each core element of life requires time and money (the financial impact will be addressed in the next chapter). You should master each core component before you decide to open the next. Each of us experiences a learning curve as we open a new element, and the time it requires impacts our schedule. Some of that time is permanently increased and some is just temporary, as that associated with any learning curve. Learning to incorporate each new element into your life as effectively as possible is the key to protecting yourself from negative levels of time stress.

The most significant misstep you can make (next to addiction or committing a serious crime) is to have a child before you start your career or a committed relationship/marriage. Children require a significant amount of time to properly parent. By having a child before you've established other core life elements (in other words, having a child "out of order"), you will not have as much time to dedicate to advancing your career or intimate relationship. This means that you will not have the finances to allow for certain conveniences and luxuries in your life. You will likely only be able to afford the bare necessities, and this can lead to frustration and feelings of always being behind the curve.

Teenagers Know Everything

Did you think you knew everything when you were a teenager? I know I did. The reason is that as a teenager, you have all 168 hours of your week to dedicate to yourself—*and* be practically free of financial stress. A teenager's matrix of life looks like this:

Life becomes significantly more complex after you move out of your parents' house, start being financially responsible, and begin having the commitments of a career, spouse, maintaining a house, and raising children. As a teenager (or for any parents of teenagers), having a basic understanding of the core elements of life and how to order them properly will help smooth out this transition to adulthood.

Summary

Since time is such a finite and perishable resource, it is important that we all manage our 168 hours each week in the most effective way possible. What we choose to do with this time is what differentiates each of us. Detailed explanations that will help you maximize your effort in each of the core elements of life are included in chapters 5 through 10. A summary of the most important ways to reduce your time stress are as follows:

- You only have 168 hours in a week. The people in your peer group that get ahead have learned how to use this precious commodity in the most effective way.
- You can do anything, but you can't do everything.
- Open one core element of life at a time. Once mastered, you are ready for the next.

- When you get married, work as a team so that you can reduce duplication of effort.
- Teenagers "know" everything because their life is at the most simple stage.

Following is a graphical depiction of time. When managed the right way, time is a valuable resource. When you overcommit your 168 hours, however, time becomes a constraint resulting in stress.

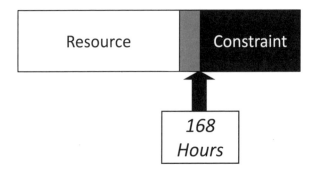

With a solid understanding of time and how precious it truly is, the second form of stress—financial—needs to be evaluated in order to make sure money (or the lack thereof) does not impede your success and happiness.

CHAPTER 4:
FINANCIAL STRESS

What do food, shelter, transportation, and vacation all have in common? They all cost money. If both the necessities and luxuries of life cost money, why do so many people disregard the importance of having finances in order? I am amazed by the sheer number of people who do not adequately manage their personal finances. It may be true that money will not make you happy, but the *lack* and *mismanagement* of money will undoubtedly make you miserable. Understanding money, its purpose, and the process of managing it is surprisingly simple. In this chapter you will learn:

- The origin and purpose of money
- How much money you can expect to earn in your life

- How to best manage your expenses
- How to prepare a budget
- The importance of saving for your retirement

Before we get into the logistics of managing personal finances, it is important to understand why money exists in the first place. I often hear people complain that if there were no financial system set in place, there would not be nearly as many problems in the world. Actually, if it were not for our monetary system, our society would, in fact, be nowhere near as evolved. And here is why.

In simpler times—centuries and empires ago—people used a barter system to acquire the necessities of life. For example, farmers would pay for supplies that they could not make or grow with bushels of their own crops. Hunters would trade excess pelts for their necessary items. Fishermen would trade excess catches for clothing or various foods. This was an extremely cumbersome and inefficient process, not to mention that the items they were trading were often perishable, which meant that they needed to constantly replenish their stores in order to continue trading goods. The time commitment and inefficiency of this type of simple bartering system is the reason why no "significant" society in human history has maintained a system like this. In order to solve the problem of using perishable goods as currency, precious metals were soon utilized in their place.

It was the ancient Greeks who, around 700 BC, stumbled upon a good use for these precious metals. They took the metals and turned them into coins. The coins, being smaller, were much more portable, but they did present a problem when dealing with larger transactions. When European trading expanded, for example, tradesmen needed a high volume of coins to complete large transactions. This is why the British, in particular, created bills of exchange.

These bills of exchange were based on precious metals held on deposit. For example, the monetary unit of the British pound was originally a unit of measure equal to one pound of silver. This system is the foundation for what we use today all over the world. Our current system has also made money more efficient and safer to store. This financial evolution of tracking and trading resources using money enables human society to move faster because people can develop an expertise in a narrow range of skills rather than dedicating a lot of time to become functional in a broad range of skills. This system allows the best people at a task to do that task as much as possible. A society of people who do a limited number of tasks exceptionally well will always produce dramatically more than a society of people who are functional at a high number of tasks. In fact, if you look at any great society or empire in history, one of the common traits is that these groups of people possessed the best method of tracking and managing resources of their time and finances.

Although some people believe our society has become too materialistic, there is one fact that remains the same today as it did for the cavemen. If you don't work hard and produce a lot of what you are good at, you will have trouble putting food on your table.

The following points demonstrate why money is such an important ingredient for the successful functioning of our society.

Yes, It Is *All about the Money*

Many people complain about the role of money in our society. Unfortunately, the fact is that money is required for every product or service in our lives, even though you may not be aware of where the money is coming from. I would like to use this as an opportunity to set the record straight:

- Insurance is *not* free. Insurance is intended to spread the cost of a catastrophic event over time. If you do not pay any insurance, you should not expect to be covered when that catastrophic event occurs (and it will!).
- What is a life worth? Until this question is answered, our health care and Medicare systems will continue to spiral out of control. In addition to the ridiculous judgments from excessive lawsuits, the reason for high health care costs is due to the fact that people are living longer and expensive technology has enabled us to save many lives that we could not previously. A century ago, the $5,000 problem would kill you. Fifty years ago, it was the $20,000 problem that would kill you. Twenty

years ago, it was the $100,000 problem. Ten years ago the $250,000 problem would kill you. Now it is the $1 million problem that finally kills you (along with a lot of prescription medications). Our medical system is capable of so much. The problem is that people are expecting coverage even though they have not paid adequately into the system.

* Another issue when it comes to our health care system is the number of medications available. A century ago there was nothing but home remedies that were generally ineffective. Today, there are so many medications. Some people take more pills on a daily basis than children eat M&Ms. No wonder why the drug companies have built up so much cash on their balance sheets.

* Now that people are living longer, they are putting a tremendous strain on the Social Security system. As people live longer, they keep cashing social security checks.

* Those with money are taken care of first. If you don't like this fact, get off the couch and work harder. Every service costs money. If you don't pay enough, why should you expect to get the same level of service as those who do pay?

* Want good service? Be a good customer! This requires you to pay your bills in full and on time.

Pay Taxes . . . and a Lot of Them

Public education, police, welfare programs, military, social security, Medicare, building roads, going to Mars, and so on. Have you ever wondered where all the money comes from to fund these programs? The money comes from taxes—taxes on our income, property, and consumer goods (or sales tax).

A relative of mine once said to me, "I paid $1,800 in taxes last year. That is ridiculous. I didn't get $1,800 worth of value from the government. Make the rich people pay!"

Being an accountant, this irritated me, but I also understood that she did not see the big picture. I asked her if someone who made $1 million last year and paid $350,000 in taxes would feel like they got value, to which she said, "I never thought of it that way." The point is this: Make money and pay taxes. The more you make, the more you will pay. The more everyone pays, the more taxes will go down. Everyone needs to pull their own weight, not just the wealthy.

If You Have Money, You Can Walk Away from Bad Situations More Easily

Gain control over your destiny and make sure you have a paycheck that covers your expenses, plus a little extra. Rely on yourself to set money aside so you do not start living from paycheck to paycheck. You will never be able to get ahead financially or plan for the future while living from paycheck to paycheck. You also want to avoid relying on the government to take care of you. The government is similar to our personal lives: It can take care of as much as it can afford. If the government runs short on money, it has two options—raise taxes or cut spending. If you have a job but you are not saving any money, you are one bad event (unexpected expense or job loss) away from being financially stressed for the foreseeable future. If you build up a decent nest egg, however, you will have more latitude to walk away from situations that compromise your values, reputation, or career without fear of being in financial straits.

Does your boss want you to cut corners? Is your employer profiting from destructive goods or services? With a cushion of savings for six months of living expenses, you have freedom to think about these issues without being distracted by the financial trade-offs of leaving your current job, if that is what you are considering. Of course, many wealthy individuals, from steroid-guzzling baseball players to corrupt politicians, make self-destructive decisions. But their financial cushion allows them to redeem or reverse their mistakes with less financial stress and to start fresh.

This principle is also applicable to our careers. Always make sure that the company you work for is a profitable one. When a company is not profitable, it will need to make difficult decisions that may cost you your job—sending you into financial woes. In all cases—but especially if your company is not financially sound—always make sure that you are earning your paycheck regardless of what those around you are doing. This may make all the difference in the world in a company that needs to downsize and has to consider which employees are helping to keep the company afloat and which are not.

The Big Three

One of the largest problems facing our society is the high level of personal debt. There are three primary reasons for this:

- The overuse of credit cards
- Financing a car that is too expensive
- Purchasing a home that is too large

With personal credit cards, you must be in a position to pay off the balance each month or you will find yourself in debt, paying outrageous interest rates that limit your cash flow in the future. You also need to save each month in case of emergencies . . . they will happen!

When it comes to what they drive, many people spend way beyond their means for vehicles that are overloaded with whistles and bells. When buying a car that is too expensive, you are limiting your financial flexibility to handle unexpected costs in the future, which will force you to increase balances on your credit cards that charge a very high interest rate. Buying a car is an opportunity to be a smart consumer, and you can do yourself a big favor by sticking with facts and reality, rather than signing up for the myths sold by advertisers, movies, and car companies designed to persuade you to self-soothe your stress via your bank account. You can save thousands of dollars by embracing another American tradition—that of being a savvy, smart consumer!

If you can avoid the American tradition of falling in love with a brand-new car, you will save a lot of money. It is important to take into consideration that a car depreciates in value the most in the first year. The last two cars I bought were two years old when I purchased them, and because of this, I saved almost 50 percent from what they would have cost me had I purchased them new. They were both fully loaded with all the options; the only thing they were missing was that new car smell. Nowadays, if you are craving that smell, you can just buy the fragrance!

Make sure you do thorough research before you set foot in a car dealership. I assure you that the dealership certainly has done theirs, and they know that your emotions are likely to override sound financial sense, especially for those who are underprepared. There are so many online resources today that can help you to learn more about purchasing cars. Know what you can feasibly pay and fall in love with that dollar amount, not the car. Remember Vernon's car story in chapter 1. Entertain vehicles out of your price range at your own peril—it is a slippery slope, and before you know it, you will have talked yourself into an upgrade. Stay focused! The best reality check is to look at the cost of the vehicle as the purchase price *plus* the full interest cost. Now instead of the sticker price of $30,000, the *real cost to you* over five years is $39,000.

The same rule applies when purchasing a home. When you are considering a home purchase, keep in mind the substantial costs you will incur over and above the base mortgage payment. You will be responsible for property taxes, electricity, heating fuel, insurance, water, repairs/maintenance, and the unexpected small damages that insurance does not adequately cover. Many never add these extra expenditures to the PITI (principal, interest, taxes, and insurance). Again, resist the emotional and status appeals used by many real estate agents to convince you of what you can and cannot afford. Never confuse the amount the mortgage lender presents as what you can afford with what you actually can pay. In many cases, this may be hundreds of dollars per month more than your actual number. Buying beyond your means is like taking the brakes off your bike before you ride down a steep hill. The ride is exciting but the consequences could be disastrous. Leave the brakes on.

Many people make the mistake of using all of their savings for their down payment when buying a home. The problem you have once you buy a home is that you then need to fill it. Furnishing a home is very expensive and you must have patience. Many people purchase the furnishings too quickly, which increases their credit card balances and puts them under tremendous financial pressure. The nuances of owning a home are discussed further in chapter 9.

By being conscious of and staying away from these "Big Three" and paying your bills on time, you will be able to protect your credit score. Your credit score is a complex calculation that rates what kind of credit risk you are based on your past financial performance. The higher your score is, the lower your risk of nonpayment. Many companies rely on this credit score to set the rates that they charge you (insurance rates, credit card interest rates, mortgage rates, and auto loan rates, to name a few). Therefore, the more you stay within your means, the cheaper everything will be for you. This is a significant reason why people who enter the realm of financial stress find it very difficult to leave. It is hard to put the brakes on the bike in mid-ride!

The Process of Understanding Financial Stress

The key to understanding financial stress is to recognize that there is a financial process put into place. As you understand this process, you will be able to manage it and avoid the stress that plagues so many people. The first step of the financial process is to understand your current earnings and earnings capacity. An important element of realizing your earnings capacity is to understand why people make what they do. Your income is based on your chosen field, education level, number of people managed, years' experience, and how many hours you work. You will learn how to control these factors to maximize the amount you will earn. As long as you have to work, why not make as much money as you can? In the long run, you want to set yourself up for future promotions, which will then lead to salary increases and a higher level of financial success.

Here is why the nice shiny bike needs brakes before you start riding down the hill. Once you understand how much you make now and calculate your potential earnings in the future, the next step in the financial process is for you to understand how much you can spend without coming into debt. If you are spending more than you make, you are in financial trouble. You have, essentially, removed the brakes. That means that you must adjust your lifestyle and start cutting expenses today. Some ways of doing so include:

- Stop eating out.
- Cut down your spending on entertainment.
- Stave off buying new clothes and be content with the ones you currently own.
- Stop furnishing your house. A bed, kitchen table, couch, and a TV are all you really need, anyway.

The final step to making sure that you keep your financial stress to a minimum is to start saving for your retirement. You cannot rely on Social Security because it will *not* be enough to continue your lifestyle into retirement. Social Security is also facing unprecedented demands as the baby boomer generation retires. The way Social Security benefits are paid out is on a graduated scale. This means that if you make $30,000 per year, you may receive almost 50 percent of your salary in Social Security when you retire. As you make more, this percentage goes down. For example, according to the IRS calculator, if you make $200,000 per year, your Social Security will be less than 15 percent of that amount. One of the biggest surprises for me was when I received my first Social Security statement and I saw that the government considered my full retirement age to be sixty-seven. What happened to sixty-five?

You should seek professional financial planning advice on your retirement and *start early*. If you do not have access to a professional, seek out the advice of someone who does use one. The longer you wait, the harder it is to build your retirement nest egg because you need compounding interest to work for you. Underfunding of retirement will be a major problem as the baby boomers begin to retire and in the years following. Spending to "keep up with the Joneses" has permanently impaired many people's ability to continue their current lifestyle into retirement.

As you manage your financial progress, keep in mind that when you are in debt, there are only two ways to get your finances under control—increase your income or decrease your expenses. It is really that simple!

In summary, and it is worth repeating again, money will not make you happy, but the *lack* of money and poor financial management *will* cause you (and your family) financial stress that will, in most cases, make you miserable.

Understand Your Earnings Potential

In this section, we will focus on the components that lead to increasing your earnings potential. When it comes to making money, you must focus on at least one of the following:

- Develop a distinctive skill for which people are willing to pay—learn how to make yourself irreplaceable.
- Manage as many other people as you can.
- Work hard.
- Sell high dollar items/services or sell a high volume.

To help you understand the factors that influence how much money you will make, I have developed the Earnings Potential Calculator (EPC). The EPC is included on the following page (a more user-friendly version is available at TheSuccessGift.com). The EPC quantifies key factors to help you understand and estimate your earnings potential. The key factors that dictate your earnings potential are:

- Education
- Chosen field
- Level of management
- Years of experience
- Number of hours per week you work
- Your "Personal Luck Potential"

Earnings Potential Calculator

Average annual income in U.S.*	$	37,500

Education level	1.00
Chosen field	1.00
Number of levels managed	1.00
Years of experience at level	1.00
Number of hours worked per week	1.00

ADJUST THESE FACTORS BASED ON THE TABLES BELOW TO SEE THE IMPACT ON YOUR EARNINGS POTENTIAL.

Expected Earnings Potential	$	37,500

Education Level:

0.45	Did not graduate from high school
0.50	High school graduate
0.70	Junior college degree
0.90	4-year college degree
1.20	Masters degree & JD
1.60	Doctorate degree

Chosen Field:

2	0.80	Not-for-profit organization
	0.90	Government and public sector
	1.00	General business
3	1.30	Professional (Accountant, Lawyer)
2	2.00	Doctor (general practitioner)
3	6.00	Doctor (specialist)
4	0.75	Retail sales (assumes a H.S. degree)
4	1.00	Low-level professional sales (4yr degr)
4	2.50	Mid-level professional sales
4	5.00	Complex professional sales
1	2.50	Banking
2	4.50	Investment Banking/Venture Capital

Number of Levels Managed:

1	1.00	No employees managed
1	1.30	1 level managed (Supervisor)
1	2.00	2 levels managed (Manager)
1	3.50	3 levels managed (Director)
2	5.00	4 levels managed (Vice President)
2	10.00	5 levels managed (COO, CFO, CMO)
2	20.00	6 levels managed (President)

Years of Experience at Level:

1.00	Less than two years
1.15	Between three and five years
1.30	Between six and ten years
1.40	Greater than 10 years

Number of Hours Worked per Week (Salaried):

0.80	35-39 hours per week
0.90	40-44 hours per week
1.00	45-49 hours per week
1.10	50-59 hours per week
1.20	60-69 hours per week
1.30	70+ hours per week

Number of Hours Worked per Week (Hourly):

0.80	35-39 hours per week
0.90	40-44 hours per week
1.00	45-49 hours per week
1.30	50-59 hours per week
1.60	60-69 hours per week
2.00	70+ hours per week

1 - *Level requires at least a 4-year college degree and Luck (See Appendix II)*
2 - *Level requires at least a Masters or JD degree and Luck (See Appendix II)*
3 - *Level requires a Medical Doctorate*
4 - *Sales is one of the few fields where you can make dramatically more without having to manage people*

* - Based on information disclosed by the U.S. Census Bureau in their press release dated August 30, 2005.

Note that if you are paid hourly, the way to estimate your current annual salary so that you can compare it to your earnings potential is to multiply your hourly rate by 2,000 (the number of work hours in a typical year). If you are paid a salary, the way to understand your hourly rate is to divide your salary by 2,000 hours.

Education

Education is the most controllable factor you have for laying a foundation that will have a significant impact on your future earnings potential. Education is an important early indicator of potential because future success is based on continually learning and improving—doing well in school helps us learn how to learn. Good students show a better aptitude for respect and continue this process throughout their careers.

High school students must focus on getting good grades and going to college if they wish to increase their chances of achieving financial success. Completing college will mean starting at a higher salary when you begin your career. In many companies and organizations, the lack of a four-year college degree will exclude you from numerous promotions and opportunities as your career progresses. In addition to a four-year degree, it is becoming more of a requirement to receive a master's degree (in business), a JD (for lawyers), or an MD (for doctors) to be truly financially successful. According to the U.S. Census Bureau, workers eighteen and over with a high school diploma earn $27,915 per year. This jumps to $51,206 for those with a bachelor's degree. This increases again to $74,602 for those with an advanced degree.

College does not guarantee financial success, of course, but it can certainly preclude it. During the process of writing this book, I decided to survey twenty-five of my closest successful friends to see if I could identify any particular trends in their level of education and their current salaries. I discovered several interesting trends that I identify throughout this book. As it pertains to college degrees, I discovered that only 8 percent did not have at least a four-year college degree. Approximately 40 percent of high school graduates will attend college and roughly half of those will receive at least a four-year degree. That means that approximately 20 percent of the population has a four- year degree, but 92 percent of financially successful people from my survey have a four- year degree. Is this just a coincidence? I think not!

If you do not receive your college degree, how can you become financially successful? Let's look at the people who I surveyed who did not have a college degree. They all had a few things in common. They developed valuable technical skills early in their careers, in areas such as Information Technology. In addition to these skills, they possessed strong social skills and worked more hours than their peers. This is important so I will summarize. If you do not have a college degree, you need the following to compensate in order to achieve financial success:

- Learn a valuable technical skill or trade.
- Develop strong social skills.
- Work long and hard.
- Become a great manager.
- Be entrepreneurial.

When it comes to education, you should put the odds in your favor by getting a good education if you want to be financially successful.

Chosen Field

Certain industries and types of jobs pay more than others. When choosing a field, make sure you know what type of lifestyle you would like to have. If you desire an expensive lifestyle, certain fields of employment simply won't pay enough no matter how long or hard you work. Also, understand the level of education required to enter your field of interest. Certain fields can only be entered if you have an adequate level of education—a bachelor's degree and often times even a master's or PhD. This is an additional reason why education is so important.

I have found that too many people pursue careers based on their academic (or recreational) interests while in high school. My dad always used to tell me, "Don't confuse your vocation with your avocation." What he meant by this is that it's important to select a career that will maximize your earnings based on your strengths— and not solely based on your likes or interests. You have your free time to pursue your personal interests if they do not match your career choice.

Early in my career, my clients were in various industries, and I found each industry fascinating. I am sure that in high school no one aspires to work for a company that manufactures toilet seats. As you understand the business as to how the toilet seats are designed, manufactured, marketed, and sold, however, it is absolutely fascinating how sophisticated that business can be. With the right mind-set, you can enjoy the nuances and challenges in any industry, even if you were not instantly drawn to it.

Side note: Develop a valuable skill and then involve your passion. Vernon, luckily, found his avocation within his vocation. After almost twenty years in financial services, he discovered that coaching and teaching others was his passion—and his talent. By the time he was ready to start a company that utilized the skill sets he both loved and excelled at, he had amassed plenty of business experience and an MBA. I, in turn, became an accountant and then went to work in the front office for a professional sports team. I made significantly more money by bringing outside expertise to the industry rather than trying to develop skills within the industry. The cruel fact of working in an industry that is highly competitive is that many people are vying for these entry- and mid-level positions. Therefore, those industries, such as professional sports, pay their employees very little (and people are willing to take lower salaries for an opportunity they have always dreamed of). It is a simple matter of supply and demand.

Level of Management

One important point to remember: your managerial "title" is not as important as how many people (and at what level those employees are at) you oversee. The compensation that comes along with any particular title can also vary widely depending on the size of a company; thus, if you are an associate manager of sales in a company where only five employees are hired, you will most likely earn less than an associate manager of sales at a large corporation where you would be managing more people.

If you have not developed a highly paid skill, such as being a cardiologist, then one of the best ways to achieve financial success is by managing others. This factor in the Earnings Potential Calculator shows how dramatically this type of promotion can impact your income. This is also why I have dedicated so much time on the topic of managing effectively in chapter 7.

Years of Experience

This factor is important when you have ten or fewer years of experience. Once you have achieved ten years of experience at a certain level, many professions do not consider it to be an incremental value, so you will tend to stay at a static income from that point forward.

Additionally, people with greater than ten years in one position are putting themselves at tremendous risk. So many companies go through downsizing initiatives at some point. People with over ten years of experience in one position who lose their jobs often have the most difficulty finding a new job in the same field. The modern business environment requires you to be flexible and to constantly enhance your skill set.

Number of Hours Worked

There is no substitute for hard work, especially early in your career. If you want to be financially successful, you must be willing to work long and hard. Challenging projects that help differentiate you from your peers rarely happen between 9:00 AM and 5:00 PM. Your working forty hours per week does not necessarily get you ahead of your colleagues.

As proof of this I would like to refer back to my survey. The most successful people from my survey worked over seventy hours per week while in their twenties to get ahead. If you are not willing to work at least fifty hours per week, you should not expect to achieve the financial success you are seeking. Additionally, you must be willing to travel, which is additional time that is not factored into that fifty hours.

The United States is the land of equal opportunity, not equality. When you honestly observe those who have taken advantage of this opportunity, a common trait is that they work long and hard. If you are not willing to make the personal sacrifice to work hard and to show your dedication to your job, you should not have the expectation of a higher income and complete financial success.

Luck?

Many people have the tendency to discount other people's success as luck. Let's take this opportunity to explore the concept of luck, its various elements, and how we can control it to our benefit. To demonstrate luck, I would like to share the story of how I became the chief financial officer for two professional sports teams. This is a job that many people would covet, and I have come across quite a few people who claim I was "lucky" to get it.

In 1993, I moved to Texas from New Jersey; at the same time, the Minnesota North Stars relocated down south and became the Dallas Stars. I was working as a senior accountant with Price Waterhouse (now known as PricewaterhouseCoopers). It was there that I discovered the Dallas Stars was a client of Price Waterhouse. Upon hearing this, I researched who the person in charge of the client was and set up a meeting with him. I informed him that I had started playing hockey when I was four while living in Canada and that he needed to put me on the client because I was one of the few people in Texas who, at the time, completely understood ice hockey.

Initially, I was not sure I would be granted this change in clients, as I was committed to the office's largest client at that time. However, I went back to my boss and presented a plan as to how I could handle the Stars engagement without allowing his client to suffer. This required working additional overtime for which I was not compensated, since I was a salaried employee. He awarded me the opportunity to take on the Stars due to my foresight and problem-solving skills.

On the Stars engagement, I became good friends with someone who was also on the Texas Rangers engagement. In July 1995, he called me at six o'clock one night and asked me if I had any plans for the evening. My wife was traveling and we did not have children at the time, so I told him I was available. He presented me with an extra ticket for a gala before the Major League Baseball All-Star Game. I hopped in my car and drove at warp speed to Six Flags in Arlington, Texas.

This was the single greatest event I have ever attended. I had a blast talking to fellow Demon Deacon (Wake Forest University alumnus) All-Star pitcher Erik Hanson. Then I found myself standing next to Pudge Rodriguez, both of us holding four-foot-long oversized stuffed killer whales and feeling like idiots. After that, I could not resist the opportunity to give Cherokee Parks a hard time because he went to archrival Duke University. During the course of the evening, my friend introduced me to the CFO for the Texas Rangers. I talked with him and the assistant controller for about an hour, and we enjoyed one another's company. At one point, the assistant controller wanted a basketball, so I said I would win her one (which actually Raul Mondesi did for me . . . thanks, Raul!). To cap everything off I was able to buy two tickets that became available at the last minute to the All-Star game the next day from the assistant controller. The seats were five rows behind home plate!

A few months later, I heard that the controller job for the Texas Rangers was open. Many people suggested I should submit my résumé. I did not, because my career at Price Waterhouse was going well and the ballpark was over an hour from where I lived. Then, out of the blue, the Texas Rangers' CFO called me directly. This changed everything, and I met with him. As I look back on my interview, my acceptance of the subsequent job offer, and my many years of employment there, I realize that this CFO was one of the best bosses I've ever had and I'm grateful to him for the opportunity he allowed me.

The job was difficult at the beginning because the accounting department was impacted by the financial strain and refund chaos caused by the players' strike in late 1994 and early 1995. I was also the first CPA hired by the Texas Rangers, so closing out the 1995 financial records required many long weeks and was, to be blunt, pure hell!

In 1996 we made various departmental improvements and efficiencies. However, whenever you make improvements, you need to allot additional time to see them through to completion. Also during this time, my wife and I had our first child. My wife was very understanding of my work commitment, however, and supported me in terms of the additional time that I spent at the office. To compensate for this, she took some time off from work. When she did go back to work, she reduced her workload, which meant she also reduced her income. Fortunately, my salary had grown as a result of my hard work, and that compensated for the decrease in my wife's income.

As the company continued to improve, the investors in the Rangers decided it was the right time to sell the club. During this process, an industry specialist from Bear Sterns stated that we had the strongest financial reporting of any team he had ever seen. When Tom Hicks bought the team, he decided to merge the front offices of the Texas Rangers with the Dallas Stars (he already owned them).

The Dallas Stars management team "won" virtually all the top management positions, except for the financial function, as a compliment to the hard work of the Rangers' accounting department. My boss, who was also responsible for operations of Rangers Ballpark in Arlington, was promoted to executive vice president of finance and operations for Southwest Sports Group. This enabled my promotion to vice president of finance of Southwest Sports Group with CFO responsibilities for the Texas Rangers and Dallas Stars.

As I reflect back on this story, was I lucky? Not necessarily. My promotion was the result of the following:

- Recognizing change early on when the Minnesota North Stars relocated
- Establishing contacts to find out key information early
- Taking the initiative to pursue my interest
- Expanding my personal network
- Working additional hours at no extra pay to handle the additional responsibilities
- Making good decisions in the workplace
- Demonstrating my qualifications by doing a good job
- Developing good relationships with people quickly by leveraging strong social skills
- Dedicating effort over a long period of time to cultivate success and not expecting immediate results
- Sacrificing time with my family

- Working with my wife as a team to allocate the time necessary to take advantage of an important and life-changing opportunity

So was I "lucky"? The answer is *no*, I was not lucky. What people generally see as luck was actually the culmination of a variety of factors. On page 63 I provide a Personal Luck worksheet so that you can calculate your own luck (a user-friendly, printable version is available at TheSuccessGift.com). There are some factors you can control and some you cannot. You must work hard to improve the factors you can control. The elements that comprise luck are as follows:

Non-controllable:

- **Intelligence**—This is an interesting element because you do not need to be twice as smart to make twice as much money. This effect is similar to professional athletes' salaries. Alex Rodriguez was not five times better at short stop than Royce Clayton when the Texas Rangers signed him to the $250 million contract, but the marginal difference made him that much more valuable.
- **Natural physical appearance**—Attractive people have an advantage when they use it in a humble way. It's true that attitude and confidence can have a positive (or negative) impact physical appearance.

Controllable:

- **Social skills**—People want to be around fun and interesting people. Strong social skills will also help you handle difficult situations that you will encounter more of as you are promoted into higher levels of responsibility.
- **Personal network**—Successful people leverage those they know into strong personal networks. A strong personal

network will help you solve problems efficiently and provide leads to new opportunities.

- **Ability to make good decisions**—Good decisions will yield profits and bad decisions will always have a cost to resolve them in terms of time or money. Many people are weighed down because they consistently make bad decisions.
- **Ability to make quick decisions**—The more good decisions you can make, the more profit you will generate. The barrier to making a lot of decisions is the time required to accumulate the necessary information. You will rarely have 100 percent of the information you need, and if you do, you surely wasted a tremendous amount of time getting it. You need to work on accumulating just enough information to make a good decision while at the same time spending as little time as possible on that effort. A good decision today is often better than the best decision tomorrow.
- **Professional appearance**—In order to play the game you must wear the uniform and abide by the rules. This means that you need to dress appropriately, act properly, and always use proper grammar when communicating with others. You should dress for the position you want, not for the one you are in.
- **Work ethic**—You need to work harder and longer than your peers if you want to get ahead. Words like "it is not my job" should never be used. You need to have pride in what you do and show consistently strong performance over a long period of time to realize success.
- **Organizational skills**—Strong organizational skills will enable you to be the most efficient with your time. If you are efficient with your time, you will be able to do more than your peers in the same time frame.
- **Self-confidence/ego**—The way you carry yourself has a large impact on your career. You need to have self-confidence so that the people around you will have complete assurance that you can do the job. Additionally, you generally need a strong ego if you want to be promoted. Ego is a subtle quality that fuels most top executives.

Personal Luck Worksheet

	Category Weighting	Personal Score	Weighted Score	
Non-Controllable Factors:				
I.Q.	20%	0	0%	A
Natural Physical Appearance	10%	0	0%	B
Controllable Factors:				
Social skills	10%	0	0%	B
Personal network	10%	0	0%	B
Ability to make good decisions	10%	0	0%	B
Ability to make quick decisions	5%	0	0%	B
Professional appearance	5%	0	0%	B
Work ethic	10%	0	0%	B
Organization skills	10%	0	0%	B
Self-confidence/ego	10%	0	0%	B
	100%			
Personal Luck Potential			0%	

Personal Score Scale is as follows:

A -
10 - IQ of 160 and above
8 - IQ between 150 and 159
6 - IQ between 140 and 149
4 - IQ between 130 and 139
3 - IQ between 120 and 129
2.5 - IQ between 110 and 119
2 - IQ between 100 and 109
1.5 - IQ between 90 and 99
1 - IQ below 90

B - *Scale of 1 to 10 (10 being the highest)*

Interpretation of results:

The management level you achieve in your career will be the largest single determinant of your earnings potential. Note that in addition to Luck, you will need certain levels of education to achieve higher levels of management. Based upon your Personal Weighted Score, you can make it to the following levels of management:

0% to	49%	No employees managed
50% to	59%	1 level managed (Supervisor)
60% to	69%	2 levels managed (Manager)
70% to	79%	3 levels managed (Director)
80% to	85%	4 levels managed (Vice President)
86% to	89%	5 levels managed (COO, CFO, CMO)
90% to	100%	6 levels managed (President)

Use the worksheet to grade yourself on each of these factors to determine your luck factor—this will then be applied to your Earnings Potential Calculator, which will help indicate at what level you may be potentially promoted. This chart will help you realize that the better you do in each category directly increases how much money you can expect to make. As you perform this exercise, you will realize two important facts:

- You control many more of the factors that you can improve (70 percent) than the factors that are beyond your control (30 percent).
- Natural physical appearance is not as significant as some people believe it is. Your intelligence and your ability to improve your performance are far more significant in your career over time.

Then there is *dumb luck*. A good example of dumb luck is winning the lottery. The odds of winning the lottery are around 1 in 20 million. Yes, somebody does win from time to time and it is fun to dream of winning. In fact, when the lottery gets over $20 million I always buy $2 worth of tickets. I consider this entertainment, similar to watching a movie, because I think about what I would do with all that money if I actually won. The key to dumb luck is to never *rely* on it. You should never spend more money or time pursuing dumb luck than you can afford to lose.

An ironic part of dumb luck is that when people receive money due to dumb luck, they tend to spend it all and find themselves back in the same place they started.

Set High Goals to Be Financially Successful

Financially successful people set high goals for themselves. When they achieve some of their goals, they set newer and higher ones. Financially successful people have good educations, work hard, and select careers in areas where they can make money.

Warning: This warning is for people who are able to set high goals for themselves. Financial success and happiness are two separate factors. You need to set reasonable expectations relative to your goals. Consistently achieving your expectations will lead to better personal happiness. Unfortunately, many people who set high goals for themselves also set high expectations. This is why many wealthy people are chronically unhappy.

Additionally, you should not gauge your success by comparing your wealth to that of others because no matter how much you have, someone else has ten times more (unless you are Bill Gates!).

Financial success is discussed further in chapter 13.

Managing Your Personal Finances

Now that you understand what your potential earnings are and you obviously know your current income, it is time to manage your personal finances. There is an important concept to learn when you are dealing with expenses—some are controllable and some are not.

Non-controllable Expenses

Non-controllable expenses include the necessities to live your life. These fall into the following categories:

- Shelter
- Food
- Transportation
- Insurance

Although you must allow for these expenses, there are ways to manage them effectively. Renting, in the short-term, *is* cheaper than buying a home. Buying or leasing an appropriate car can also help you stay within a tight budget.

Insurance is extremely important but it is not free. The purpose of insurance is to pay a small amount on a consistent basis so that it mirrors your personal cash flow. Then, when a major problem occurs (and it will), the expense can be covered without causing you major financial difficulty. You must maintain car, health, and home insurance for catastrophic events. If you have children, it is irresponsible not to pay for life insurance. Not paying for proper insurance means that huge financial problems may be looming in the distance.

Controllable Expenses

Your other expenses are controllable, which means you can live without them. You can also manage higher or lower levels of spending depending on the month and your financial obligations. These also allow for you to have certain luxuries in your life. You need to decide what is important to you and then prioritize each item. Rarely will you ever be able to afford everything you want in life. As you increase your income, you will generally find that your material desires increase as well, so you may still not reach the level of financial success you are hoping to obtain.

Pay Off Your Credit Card Balances!

All too often people use their credit cards to buy things, thinking that they will pay off the bill the following month. Then, an emergency happens or a new pair of shoes calls your name and you are unable to pay the full amount and end up paying the minimum. Credit cards are extremely dangerous to your financial health. An example follows:

If Bob charges $500 per month on his credit card and only repays $250 per month, he will end up with the following balances:

	Purchases	Payments	Total Interest	Ending Balance
After 5 years	30,000	(15,000)	6,218	21,218
After 10 years	60,000	(30,000)	32,073	62,073
After 20 years	120,000	(60,000)	200,117	292,190
After 30 years	180,000	(90,000)	823,096	1,145,286

From one month to the next in the early years, his credit card debt will cause Bob financial trouble, but he still has a chance to change his habits. Once this goes on past five years, though, it will be almost impossible for Bob to pay off his credit card balance. His payments through year 10 approximate the interest that the credit card company has charged for that same period. This means that he is receiving *nothing* for what he is paying. This is a horrible situation to find oneself in, and unfortunately it is all too common.

Obviously between years 10 and 20, Bob would not be able to purchase anything more on his credit cards. He will, in effect, become an indentured servant to the credit card companies. The credit card companies have an interesting way of providing you with enough credit to get you into trouble but not so much that they lose money (especially with the bankruptcy laws that make declaring bankruptcy today even more difficult).

Note that the above amounts were based on a credit card interest rate of 14 percent. Many credit cards will charge you around 18 percent or more for outstanding balances, which will have an even more catastrophic effect on your personal finances.

Personal Budget Worksheet

Included on the page 69 (and at TheSuccessGift.com) is a Personal Budget worksheet that will help you manage your personal finances (and prevent the American Nightmare). You should not be intimidated by this exercise. It is extremely important to understand how to avoid financial stress, and this worksheet makes that understanding easy.

Start by filling out your income and all of your expenses. Is the bottom number positive or negative? If it is positive, you are in good shape. If it is negative, there are only two ways to make it positive:

- Increase income—This requires you to answer questions about changes that are likely difficult to implement, such as "Should I work more hours?"; "Should I get a second job?"; "Does my spouse/partner need to get a job?"; "Do I need to find another job that pays better?"

- Decrease expenses—Categorize where you are spending. Are you spending money on items such as luxuries that can easily be reduced? If you do not have categories that can easily be reduced, that is a sign that you are living a lifestyle that is too expensive for you. You also may be driving a car or living in a home that is more expensive than you need.

The key to managing budget cuts is to be sure to adjust the behavior and spending habits that result from the expense. If you do not adjust your behavior and expectations, you will continue to have financial stress. *The best indicator of financial stress is carrying a balance on your credit card from month to month.*

When you establish a budget, be sure to closely monitor your activity over a few months until you start learning the proper habits. After that, you can monitor key indicators such as:

- Has your income changed?
- Are you carrying a balance on your credit cards?
- Has the balance in your checking and/or savings account(s) come down?
- Are you hitting your savings goals?

You must actively manage your personal finances. Ignoring them will only make your financial problems worse!

Personal Budget Worksheet (monthly)

Income:
Take-home pay - husband
Take-home pay - wife
Investment income
Interest income
Expense reimbursements/allowances
Other

Total Income

Expenses:

Non-controllable:
Car payment - #1
Education loans-repayment
Insurance - auto
Insurance - life/medical/other
Medical/dental
Other
Total non-controllable exp.

Home related expenses:
Electricity
Heating fuel (natural gas/oil)
Home furnishings
Insurance - home/renters
Landscaping
Maid
Pest control
Pool service
Property taxes
Rent/mortgage
Repairs & maintenance
Telephone
TV (cable/satellite)
Water
Other
Total home-related expenses

Other controllable expenses:
Cash spending
Contributions
Gifts
Mobile phone
Other
Total controllable expenses

Credit card expenses:
Balance repayment
Car-maint/repair
Dry Cleaners
Entertainment
Gasoline
Groceries
Meals
Miscellaneous
Pets
Vacation
Other
Total credit card expenses

Spouse related expenses:
Car payment
Education loans-repayment
Additional insurance
Additional credit card spending
Additional cash spending
Mobile phone
Other
Total spouse-related expenses

Children related expenses
Daycare
Additional credit card spending
Additional cash spending
Activities and school
College savings
Other
Total children related expenses

Total Expenses:

Comfortable/(Stressed)

Special Note:
This schedule does not address saving for your retirement. Please see an expert in this area so that your personal retirement goals can be achieved. For many people, social security and contributions to a 401(k) will not be sufficient to continue their current lifestyle into retirement.

You Must Save for Retirement . . . Early

One of the best financial decisions you can make early in your career is to start saving for retirement. People who save early will have a much easier time saving for their retirement because compounding interest will be working for you. This means that in addition to what you are able to save, you will also earn interest. For example:

- Janet saves $2,000 per year from age twenty-two through thirty (only nine years).
- Bob saves $2,000 per year from age thirty-one through sixty-five (thirty-five years).
- All amounts invested earn 8 percent per year.

Who do you think will have more money at age sixty-five?

It seems like it should be Bob because he saved for thirty-five years (almost four times longer!). The interesting fact is that Janet would actually have more money at age sixty-five. This is the power of compounding interest.

Note that in this example, Janet would have almost $400,000 at retirement. This may sound like a lot to some but it is nowhere near enough for a comfortable retirement. This will only generate approximately $1,500 per month of additional income. You must consult a professional financial advisor as soon as possible (if you have not done so already) so that you can set up a plan based on your individual goals to ensure a comfortable retirement.

Always invest in your company's 401(k) savings plan. The advantages are that you use money to invest before taxes are taken out, so you don't pay income tax on the earnings until you take the money out (so more money is compounding), *and* your company usually matches a portion of the amount you are investing (they are basically giving you *free* money!).

A 2004 Gallup survey and many other sources agree: Young people are more confident about retirement than older folks. The Gallup poll found that 71 percent of eighteen- to twenty-nine-year-olds were confident they would have enough money for retirement, compared with much lower figures for other groups. This is a dangerous mind-set, however. As we mature, we almost inevitably carry additional responsibilities, from children to aging parents to owning a home. All of these require significant financial support— almost always more than you expect. Remember, most of us see our incomes drop dramatically after we reach our early fifties and then decline further as we approach retirement. It is not smart to wait until our mid-fifties to start saving for retirement because these are our toughest earning years. If we are not prepared for retirement *before* we have children or shoulder other long-term costs, we are going to fall behind. This will mean adjusting our lifestyle dramatically. It is always easier to live better later than to cut back your lifestyle in retirement because at that stage, you will likely have minimal earnings potential.

To demonstrate this point: for every $100 pair of shoes you don't buy when you are twenty-two, investing that money instead, you will have $3,000 more at age sixty-five. What would you rather have when you are sixty-five, a forty-three-year-old pair of shoes or $3,000? The best time to start saving is today!

Summary

Now that you have read about money and the financial stress the lack of it can cause, I would like to graphically illustrate how money *can* be a valuable resource. But if you spend too much, it becomes a constraint that causes unending financial stress. The point at which money becomes a constraint is different for everyone, but it is easy to know exactly where it is. It is your income!

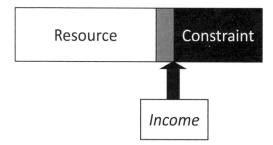

Since money is so important, let's summarize what we have learned in this chapter:

- Money is a system that was established to manage our resources and to allow us to produce extra resources using our unique skills.
- Our earnings in life are based on our education level, chosen field, number of people managed, work experience, and how long we work.
- It is important to develop a skill that others value and are willing to pay for.
- Manage expenses effectively and pay off credit card balances.
- Prepare a budget so that you know before you make any commitments that you are not subjecting yourself to financial stress.
- Start saving early for retirement.

Now that we understand how to manage time and financial stress, we can address the final category of stress in life: social stress.

CHAPTER 5:
SOCIAL STRESS

Have you ever been to a party and felt out of place among the other guests? I know I certainly have. Standing there, looking around, trying to figure out how to act, and wondering, *Who should I talk to?* How does this make you feel? Not very good, I am sure. Then, as time goes by, you either become more comfortable and you find someone to talk to or you don't become more comfortable and you feel trapped. These situations can cause a plethora of emotions and feelings to go careening through your head. Often, though, people fail to look at social stress from a process perspective; that is, what causes you to have successful social interactions and what brings out negative ones. In this chapter, you will learn:

- The sources of social groups
- Who you are and who you can be

- How the definition of "cool" changes
- Various types of relationship stress
- How to define your personal skill sets

Sources of Social Groups

Why do you choose to interact with someone at a given point in time? This is an important part of understanding how to develop social skills and friendships. Most of our interactions take place within a social circle. Social circles are established based on the following individual factors, or a combination thereof:

- Common interests
- Humor
- Athletic ability
- Physical attractiveness
- Chosen career
- Employer
- Geographic convenience (neighbors)
- Age
- Gender
- Religion
- Ethnic heritage
- Intellectual capacity
- Education level
- Financial level
- Children's friends and activities

Due to these factors, our perception of who is desirable, or "cool," to spend time with will change over time. As teenagers, we typically define our social circles (and the people who make up our friend group) by age, physical appearance, and even athletic ability. However, as we age and enter the "real world," our social circles tend to based more on where we live, where we work, our financial situations, our views, our children, and our common interests.

When thinking about your social circle, remember that peer pressure plays a key role in our interactions with others. When you surround yourself with positive people, this peer pressure can actually motivate you to achieve more than you normally might. Negative peer pressure, though, can have the exact opposite effect. This is why it is important to surround yourself with peers who have a positive impact on you.

Understand Who You Are and Who You Can Be

The best way to handle social stress is to assess your personality, interests, "turn ons," and "turn offs." Understand your strengths and weaknesses; understand your passions. Are you someone who loves solitary hobbies and interests (gardening, wood carving, or painting)? You are not likely to flourish when you're invited to a loud Sunday NFL party at a busy local pub. Are you into steam punk and skateboarding? Then head to the local skate park. If you are a flexible, curious person with wide interests, build on that strength and enjoy your wide network of friends. However, many highly social individuals make the mistake of spreading their social networks too wide and end up with many shallow relationships. Find social circles where your strengths are valued. Avoid groups who value the characteristics in which you are weak, as these groups will make you feel insecure. Be mindful that over time you—and your priorities—will change and you may very well become involved in new social circles.

You will also fall out of favor with social circles from time to time. Usually, the only thing that can fix these problems is time. That is why it is important to be involved with several social circles that are independent from each other. When you fall out of favor with one, you can easily migrate your time to another. Social circles take root where there are groups of people; our institutions and interests will form these circles. Think of your own social circles. Are they linked to any of the following?

- School
- Neighborhood
- Athletic teams
- Activities, common interests, and ethnic heritage

- Church
- Work
- Community assistance and improvement initiatives

This is a significant reason why being involved in various activities is so important for our personal well-being.

The Definition of "Cool" Changes

"Cool" is defined by *Webster's Dictionary* as fashionable or hip. When we are teenagers, "cool" can be used to describe someone who is attractive, stylish, funny, or a good athlete. As we get older, the definition of "cool" becomes much broader and can be based on being considered better or more active by people in any of the social circles identified earlier. At work, those who are "cool" may be the people who are the experts on any given topic or the people in line for the next promotion. In the neighborhood, Mr. Cool may be the one who is involved in helping the living environment in your area become better and more livable.

For those of you who were not considered cool during your middle and high school years, fear not. You have the power to become cool as you age; obtaining an education that will land you a great job and lead to maximized success and happiness will also propel you beyond your former high school athlete and prom queen counterparts who only have the "glory days" to look back on now.

Nothing is cooler when you get older than achieving *your* desired level of success and happiness!

Relationship Stress

A significant portion of our social stress as we complete our educations and begin our careers relates to our relationships with both friends and significant others. There is so much that changes between high school and college; then, change happens again when we enter the working world. There are even more changes to encounter in the real world resulting from career switches, relocations, and priority shifts, especially when you have children.

Relationships are built around common interests (i.e., geographic location, educational level, chosen major, careers, favorite activities, and how one spends his or her leisure time). When those common interests change (and they will), you will naturally gravitate to new relationships and make new friends who share those common interests. This evolution explains why it is rare that we spend as much time with old friends as we do with new ones. For me, I always know who is a true friend. It is someone I may not have talked to in months or even years but when I do, we pick up exactly where we left off.

The real challenge comes when you have a romantic relationship. Then, when a significant change or opportunity is presented, such as a job, relocation, or merging of goals, both sides will need to make sacrifices, often one side more than the other. Can your relationship handle this type of compromise? Will the sacrifice be in favor of the better opportunity or in favor of the dominant person in the relationship? The significant changes in geographic locations and general interests between high school and college, and again between college and the working world, create understandable barriers for relationships to last during these major periods of change. Major changes do not stop there, either. In the working world you will be presented with new opportunities, many requiring you to relocate to a new facility, new city, or even a new state or country. Healthy relationships are ones that enable you to take advantage of these positive opportunities. Negative relationships are ones that present a barrier for the growth of one person by the other. The more you try to control this natural process, the more frustrated and socially stressed you are sure to become.

To demonstrate this point, I would like to refer back to my survey of financially successful people. I was curious as to how many of these people met their future spouse in high school. Only 4 percent met in high school. It is interesting to think back on how much of my stress and insecurities in high school related to the opposite sex, when in reality it only had a 4 percent chance of working out.

To mitigate stress that results from relationships, make a conscious effort to continue to grow and evolve as an individual, and as a life partner or friend. Ensure that you surround yourself with people who share your goal as well. Surrounding yourself with people who are intimidated and resentful of growth and advancement will stunt your potential.

Watch Out!

There are always groups of young people or adults (you will find them at bars, at the racetrack, or at the casino) who spend most of their free time "hanging," to put it charitably, "partying" (less charitably), gambling, fighting, or doing even worse. They prey on people who are the most insecure by giving them a group that "accepts" them. In exchange, the group soothes their sense of being socially marginalized and boosts their status. This is as true of urban gangs as it is of the group that shuts down your local bar every weekend and misses a lot of Mondays due to hangovers. Marginal gangs need followers. Yes, you'll find these groups quite welcoming. They need your company. What will inevitably happen if you become involved, though, is you will be pulled down to their level. These dead-enders are intimidated by success and positive self-image. These people are well-known throughout any given community; try to steer clear of them.

The social circles you choose should encourage positive behavior. Insecure groups encourage negative behavior that can be detrimental to you for the rest of your life. People can be (and usually are) judged by the company they keep.

Personal Skill Set

Now let's think about your personal set of skills as a resource for your happiness. As you invest in your personal skills, you'll find it easier and more comfortable to choose situations where your abilities and experience are on par with your social circle. Suddenly, your social experiences are not considered a stress but rather a resource and source of satisfaction.

The key personal skills were mentioned in the Financial Stress chapter as a determining factor in your "Personal Luck Potential." They include social skills, personal network, ability to make good decisions, ability to make quick decisions, professional appearance, work ethic, organizational skills, and self-confidence. All of these skills can be developed, improved, and mastered as you mature. Even the best people in any social circle have weaknesses that they work to improve and strengths that they try to master.

Summary

Now that social stress and personal skill set has been addressed, I would like to graphically illustrate how this skill set can be a truly valuable resource when applied properly. If overcommitted, this skill set becomes a constraint resulting in stress. Even as we know it is wise to avoid stressful situations, by developing your personal skill set you reduce the number and intensity of those situations.

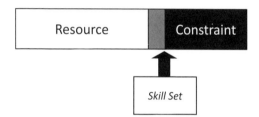

The great news is that your personal set of skills can be consistently improved and expanded throughout your lifetime. Let's summarize what you have learned in this chapter and what you need to strive for in order to allay social stressors:

- Understand how social groups are formed.
- Be honest with who you are and find a positive social group that appreciates your strengths.
- Not "cool"? Don't worry. You just haven't found the right group yet. You will have many, many options throughout your life.
- Stress resulting from a relationship with a significant other should be an indicator that you are with the wrong match.

- Continue to expand your personal skill set by improving the weaknesses and mastering the strengths.

Now that you understand how to manage the three main stresses, it is time to begin addressing each of the core elements of life.

PART II

THE CORE ELEMENTS OF LIFE

The next section of this book defines the core elements of life. They are as follows:

- Self
- Career
- Marriage/Relationship
- Home
- Children

Life today is much more complex than ever before and will only continue to be more so as the years pass. As children, we are now exposed at a very young age to very mature concepts. One result of this is that we want more than we have ever wanted before. The problem associated with this, however, is that we have less patience to cultivate and build our lives than we previously have. One can have a fulfilling life and do whatever he or she wants but he or she cannot do everything at the same time.

The following six chapters address each of the core elements of life. As mentioned earlier, the only two elements that are mandatory are self and career. All of the others are optional and will vary based on individual life experiences. It is extremely important to master each core element you have, though, prior to addressing the next core element so that a solid foundation can be built each step of the way. Order is key and of utmost importance!

Once each of the core elements of life are addressed and understood, you will then be prepared to gain a better understanding of what gives depth to our lives: happiness, financial success, and achievements.

CHAPTER 6:
SELF

Achieving the highest possible level of success and happiness starts with laying a proper foundation for oneself. One of the primary reasons I decided to write this book was that I frequently witness so many people making poor short-term decisions that will have a clear, negative effect on their lives for years to come. Let me share some insights that demonstrate the importance of building and maintaining a solid foundation for your future:

- Upon turning twenty, you will have been a teenager for 35 percent of your life and that sounds like forever.

- Assuming you die at eighty years of age, you will have only been a teenager for 8 percent of your life.
- Unfortunately, the 75 percent of your life that occurs after your teen years is heavily dependent on the decisions you made as a teenager.

Regardless of where you are on the walk of life, you cannot change what has happened. Do not let this get you down, however. We have all had challenges and have all made some mistakes. The great news is that 100 percent of the life ahead of you is based on what you choose to do today.

The following are various learning opportunities to help you with your personal life. Within each category, the points are not in any particular order because each point could be more or less important depending on your experiences and current situation. The learning opportunities that affect the core element of self are organized in such a way:

- Making good decisions
- General advice and observations
- Personal traits and habits
- Societal factors

Making Good Decisions

One day I had lunch with a former coworker. At the time, he was studying to become a minister (which he has since become). As we talked about our respective families, I learned that he had two teenage daughters. Knowing that this is a difficult stage in parenting, I asked how he and his wife handle it. He told me he focuses on helping his daughters make good decisions. He said he also works on helping them identify bad decisions when they make them, because rarely does the first bad decision get you into serious trouble. It is usually the second, third, or fourth bad decision in a row that gets you into serious trouble.

As we have discussed, understanding your goals and expectations are quite important. By identifying your ultimate goal, you can use that process to improve your decision making. Here's how:

1. Identify the general path you've discerned for your life.
2. Lay out goals and expectations to clarify that path.
3. When making decisions, consider whether the decisions bring you closer or further from achieving the goals and expectations you previously identified.
4. Listen to your inner voice and trust your natural instincts.

If you struggle with making good decisions, reach out to your network of friends or family who may have experience in a certain area or about a certain topic that you are finding difficult to decide on. Your social network and family may be able to be more objective than you can, particularly when a difficult decision needs to be made. Another way to make good decisions is to recognize bad decisions you've made in the past and actively work to avoid them in the future. We identify a likely "bad" decision as having any of these traits:

- Not based on facts
- Illegal
- Not good for your health
- Separates you further from your goals/expectations
- Causes conflict with others

Always think of the consequences of bad decisions (yes, teenagers, I know you think you are bulletproof, but you need to learn the consequences of bad decisions . . . sooner rather than later). One of the best ways to avoid making bad decisions is to stay away from people who repeatedly make bad decisions. Remember: You are judged by the company you keep, so don't associate yourself with people who are deemed bad decision makers if you don't want to be viewed as one yourself.

Two main reasons for bad decisions are boredom and rebellion. Staying busy and knowing when decisions will hurt are essential. When a bad decision is made (and they will be made at some point), the key is to recognize it and change your course or get help as soon as possible. People are quick to forgive the first bad decision you make, but they may not be as tolerant of those to follow.

The decisions you make should be classified by their relative impact. Big life decisions include where to go to college, what career to pursue, who to marry, which home to buy, and how many children to have. Small decisions include where to eat on a given evening or what movie to see. Once a decision is appropriately classified as either big or small, spend the appropriate time on it. Don't spend too little time on big decisions or spend too much time on small decisions—always consider if the decision you make will make a difference in twenty years. If so, spend a little more time considering the outcome and the possibilities before you move forward.

No one makes 100 percent correct decisions, even on big issues. Instead, focus on making more right decisions than wrong ones. Remember, even if you are fearful or nervous of making a bad decision, avoiding a decision is in itself a decision, and not likely a good one. If you are paralyzed about making a decision between two job offers, and postpone making the choice, you will, in all likelihood, decide to pass on both offers.

Allow us one final point on good decision making: you will rarely have 100 percent of the necessary information you need to fully judge what is a good and what is a bad decision. People who are most efficient with their time can make good decisions with a relatively low percentage of the necessary information. One benefit of making a good decision includes making good use of time, because it takes time to gather information, and if you can make a decision using less information than others, that means you possess more time for other tasks. The art of good decision making is using enough time—but only just enough—to gather an adequate amount of information. One of Colin Powell's enduring contributions to leadership is his observation that "once the information [you need to make a decision] is in the 40 to 70 percent range, go with your gut. Don't wait until you have enough facts to be 100 percent sure, because by then it is almost always too late."

To reinforce this concept of managing and making good decisions, I have developed a simple exercise. Use the grid below, a six-sided die, and a coin. Perform the following:

- Place the coin on the "Start" square.
- Roll the die and move according to the numbers below:
- 1 to 2: Good decision—move right one space and up one space.
- 3 to 4: No decision—stay on the same square.
- 5 to 6: Bad decision—move right one square and down one space.
- Continue this until you get to the far right.
- Where did you end up and how many rolls did it take?
- Perform this a few more times to see where you end up and take an average of where you ended and how many rolls it took.

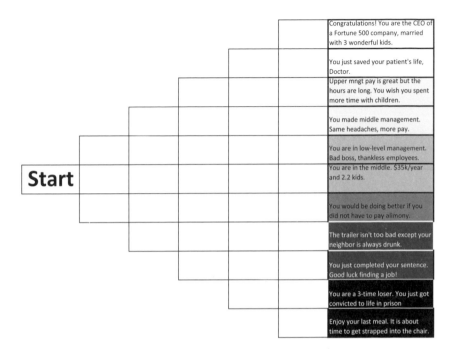

Now let's change things a little. Say that you have internalized everything in this book and you are a quick, effective decision maker who makes many more good decisions than bad. Perform the following:

- Place the coin on the "Start" square.
- Roll the die and move according to the numbers below:
- 1 to 5: Good decision—move right one space and up one space.
- 6: Bad decision—move right one square and down one space.
- Continue this until you get to the far right.
- Where did you end up and how many rolls did it take?
- Compare the results in this exercise with the results under the first set of rules. Were they the same?

Statistically, this exercise shows that people who make better decisions on a more consistent basis end up in a better place more quickly. The key is to consistently improve your decision-making abilities.

General Advice and Observations

Certain traits of ours extend beyond our own decisions and affect the well-being of people around us. Keeping these in mind will help improve the odds of success and happiness in all areas of your life, not just in this core element.

Have a Positive Attitude

Each morning, when you wake up, you have a very important decision to make: Are you going to have a positive attitude today? No single decision that is made on a daily basis is as important as choosing to have a positive attitude each and every day. People with positive attitudes will achieve far greater things and be happier in life in general than those who view the world through a negative lens on a day-to-day basis.

Accept Responsibility

It seems like we now live in a "no fault" society where many people feel they are entitled to certain things but do not have to reap the consequences of any fallout. Every time someone does something wrong or something bad happens, it is always someone else's fault. The first step toward happiness is to accept responsibility for the decisions you make (no matter what the outcome) and to understand that you are not entitled to anything simply because you exist. People who accept responsibility will feel significantly more control over their destiny. This feeling of being in control is an important part of obtaining happiness.

It's true that you can blame your parents for giving you the genetic coding that makes you the way you are; yet, you cannot blame them—or anyone else for that matter—for the decisions you choose to make. The life you lead today is comprised of many decisions you made in the past. If you've made a lot of good decisions, you are probably in a happier and more successful state than your peers who choose poorly along the path of life.

Help Others Help You

This subheading reminds me of one of my favorite jokes: One day during some torrential downpours, a neighborhood started to flood. Once the flooding started to enter a house, the man who lived there went to his raised front porch. A boat came by and the driver in the boat said, "Hop on in and I will take you to higher land." The man on the porch said, "No thank you. I am praying to the Lord and the Lord will save me."

It continued to rain and the water level got much higher so now the man had to climb onto his roof. Another boat came by and the rescuer said, "Hop on in and I will take you to higher land." The man on the roof said, "No thank you. I am praying to the Lord and the Lord will save me."

The rain continued and the water level rose even higher. Now the man had to stand on his chimney. Luckily a helicopter flew over and spotted him. The pilot threw down a rope ladder and got on the loud speaker and said, "Grab hold of the ladder and I will take you to higher land." The man on the chimney said, "No thank you. I am praying to the Lord and the Lord will save me."

Unfortunately, the rain continued, the water level rose, and the man drowned. He ascended to heaven and just before he entered the gates, St. Peter asked the man if he had any questions before entering. The man said, "I don't really have a question but I am rather disappointed."

St. Peter, shocked, asked why the man was disappointed. The man said, "I prayed to the Lord and I thought the Lord would save me." To which St. Peter replied, "Well heck, we sent you two boats and a helicopter . . . what else did you want?"

In every joke, there is usually a little bit of truth. Many people have trouble recognizing help when it is being offered. If you continue to refuse it, though, eventually people will stop offering.

Therefore, help others to help you by recognizing what is going on . . . and be appreciative when help does come your way.

Life Isn't Fair . . . So Get Over It

There are many situations that creep up in life that may seem unfair. In fact, many times these situations are unfair. However, when you are presented with this "unfair" situation, you do have a choice: you can complain about it and let it continue to bother you without action *or* you can use the situation to fuel your motivation to improve the circumstances. The irony is on the flip side of this situation. When you get something positive that others would perceive as not fair, you usually don't remember.

To demonstrate this point, let's use an example from the game of poker. I like playing Texas Hold'em with my friends from time to time. There have been several situations when I have gotten lucky cards and beat someone (this is called a "bad beat"). I rarely remember when I "bad beat" someone but I always remember when someone "bad beats" me, especially if it puts me out of the game.

Learn from Other People's Mistakes

It has always amazed me how a significant number of people feel the need to learn from their own mistakes when they could easily learn from others or notice obvious signs that could help them avoid the problematic situation. I call this *standing on bird poop*. If you stand on a pile of bird poop long enough, you will most likely find some of it landing on your head. The reason is that the birds above you are doing the same thing they always do. You need to have the common sense to know that cycles repeat themselves. By noticing the bird poop on the ground, you can assume that there are birds nesting above and you can then avoid standing underneath.

Mistakes are great learning opportunities. In fact, the mistakes we make are usually the best lessons we will ever learn. In that case, mistakes are also a little like bird poop—you sometimes have to deal with them (or you watch others deal with them) in order to learn how to overcome them in the future. If you can learn from other people's mistakes, your life will be far easier and happier.

Play the Odds

The lessons and observations I share in this book are rarely absolute. There are always exceptions to every rule or situation. Instead of taking an "I'll prove you wrong" perspective in which you expend too much time and energy learning your own lessons, just play the odds. If you believe you can attain better success by doing something (such as getting higher education), then take your changes and go for it. If you feel that you are more likely to get into trouble by acting a certain way (such as doing drugs), then play the odds and decided whether the risk is worth the potential loss.

Successful people have a proven track record of playing the odds, making good decisions, and being a strategic contrarian.

Controllable versus Non-controllable

When presented with difficult situations or decisions in your life, you must identify which aspects of the situation are within your control and which are not. Vernon and I have witnessed over and over again throughout the years how talented people waste time and energy trying to change something that is not controllable (such as their height, their ancestry, or even the economy). You must understand the limitations that the situation or decision has on you and learn to function within those limitations.

Your time is best spent when you try to change or improve controllable factors like your education, work performance, social networking, time management, money management, and the like.

Life Is as Difficult as You Want to Make It

Everyone has difficulties in their life. What you must decide is if you are going to dwell on the negative and worry about that which cannot be controlled. If you do, that is your own fault. We are all dealt a hand in life and it is our responsibility to play it the best we can.

Many people like to worry about what happened to them in the past. If you are one of those people, I suggest you read *Man's Search for Meaning* by Viktor Frankl. This is an extraordinary book in which Dr. Frankl, a psychiatrist, writes of his experience being imprisoned in a concentration camp during World War II. He was intrigued by how it was possible for some people to survive while others died, given their same horrific conditions. He surmised that the reason many people died is that they lost hope and lost sight of their goals. At the end of the war, when everyone in these camps was released, his experiences and observations while interned changed how he counseled people in the future. He would tell his clients that it does not really matter what has happened in the past. What is vastly important are your goals and what you want to achieve in the future.

Have a Good Personal Network

Six Degrees of Separation was not one of my favorite movies, but the title represents an interesting concept. It suggests that everyone in the world is, in fact, six relationships away from any other person. Using this idea, it is imperative that in your personal and business life, you establish a personal network that is either one or at most two degrees of separation from people who can help you solve problems and lead you toward success. How many degrees of separation are you from an attorney, tax accountant, IT expert, financial consultant, or someone with an excellent set of power tools?

What this all boils down to is the fact that you need to get to know as many people as possible who are in a position to help you through any crisis or situation. The best ways to do this are to:

- Get out there and meet people.
- Remember names.
- Learn something interesting about each person you meet that will help you remember them at a later date.
- Listen to people while they talk.
- Tell interesting, funny, and relevant stories and jokes.
- Maintain eye contact.
- Have a firm handshake (nothing is worse than throwing someone a dead fish).
- Smile, be fun-loving and interesting, so that you, as well, will be memorable to others in the future.

Collect Favors

Once your personal network is expanded, you must now figure out how to maximize the benefit of such a group of peers. Simple: favors. Whenever someone asks you for help, there are only three possible replies: "yes," "sure," or "no problem." Many people are so interested in what someone can do for them that they forget the important part of relationships is what you can do for others. Helping others will go a long way toward making you—and your acquaintances—happy. An interesting result is that the more you help other people, the more eager they are to help *you* when you need it.

How do you think I was able to get this book published?

Asking for Help versus Telling People What to Do

No matter what the situation is or whether someone owes you a favor or not, always *ask* for help. People generally enjoy helping others. On the other hand, no one likes to be told what to do, so don't get into the habit of bossing people around—you will be less likely to find help at a future time if this is how you consistently interact with others.

There Are Different Types of IQ

Generally, people are smart—just in different ways. Being smart in one way does not make you smart in every way. Understand your strengths and weaknesses; once you know your strengths, exploit them to your advantage. Conversely, once you understand your weaknesses, work to improve these.

Winning Is Easy . . . How You Handle It Is Not

In our competitive society, a tremendous amount of focus is placed on winning. Sometimes we are taught to win at all costs or that winning is the only option. As we age, there are a few additional concepts that we learn in terms of winning. First, win gracefully. An opponent who gets embarrassed will harbor ill will and want revenge if he sees you gloating over your victory. Second, as competition follows you off the playing field and into other parts of your life (i.e., relationships or business), seek win-win interactions with your opponents. If you negotiate to the point where you win all and the other person loses all, be sure that this will haunt you at a later date—and usually at an inopportune time. Finally, when you do win, always allow your opponent to save face. You will build many allies and expand your network if you handle these types of interactions appropriately.

The key, though, is to always seek win-win solutions in every confrontation you encounter.

It Takes a Lifetime to Earn Trust

It takes a lifetime to earn trust and only one moment to lose it. Once lost, trust is incredibly difficult to earn back. Trust is a precious commodity that must not be taken lightly. At the end of the day, we are only worth our word. Make sure that your word is always considered valuable and trustworthy.

Personal Traits and Habits

During my work experiences I have noticed several traits and habits of people that should be pointed out. Many of these are traits of successful people and some are common mistakes and negative traits that you should avoid at all costs.

Do the Right Thing

You will have many opportunities throughout your life to take advantage of certain situations. It is important to always have your moral compass pointing in the right direction. The main way to test this is whether or not you do the right thing when nobody is watching. When you train yourself to always do the right thing, you will never find yourself in a situation where you've lied and cannot cover it up or where you have done a misdeed and now must account for your actions.

You possess integrity when you do the right thing even when no one is watching.

Never Lose Your Sense of Humor

We all will, inevitably, encounter difficult situations in our lifetime. It is very important to always maintain a sense of humor and a positive attitude, even in the most trying of situations. People always want to be around fun-loving, happy, and interesting people. If you lose your sense of humor or you are easily offended, you will not be able to expand your personal network as wide as it needs to be in order to make the necessary contacts for future endeavors, and you will never realize your full potential.

Treat Others the Way You Want to Be Treated

This reminds me of another one of my favorite jokes: During the Vietnam War, there were two officers who employed a Vietnamese houseboy to take care of all the cleaning, cooking, errands, and whatnot. These two officers became bored one day and decided to play jokes on the boy to amuse themselves and to help pass the time. The amazing thing about this boy is that no matter how inappropriate or cruel the officers' jokes were, he would always keep a smile on his face and maintain a positive attitude.

After several weeks of playing tricks on the boy, the officers started feeling guilty. They brought the boy into the living room and had him sit down. They apologized to the boy and said that they would not play any more tricks on him. The boy said in broken English, "You play no more tricks?" They promised that the tricks would stop. He inquired again for reassurance, "No more?" And the officers convinced him that they were serious.

At that point, the boy said, "Okay then . . . I stop pissing in soup."

The point to be made here is to always treat others well. You will reap what you sow and others will treat you the way you treat them. If you treat someone poorly, the question you should ask yourself is, "How are they getting back at me?"

It is important, as you go through life, that you always treat others as you would like to be treated. When you are in a situation with someone else and you are not sure how to act, simply put yourself in the other person's shoes—which can be easier said than done but is important nonetheless.

Now that I have reminded you to always be nice to others, I also want to make sure you have a backbone and a thick skin. Some people will try to take advantage of nice people like you. Make sure that you recognize these people and distance yourself from them. Some people can be an absolute drain on your time, resources, and energy—and some can even go so far as to try to sabotage your success and happiness.

Speak the Language . . . Properly

Language is a common denominator in any society. This means that, in the United States particularly, you must speak English (or the language you are doing the most business in) properly in order to be successful. Poor grammar and ineffective communication skills not only project a sense of being uneducated but it can also limit your effective business transactions with clients and customers. Keep in mind that you are constantly making an impression on the people you interact with. You do not have a second chance to make a good first impression, so do not let poor speaking abilities taint your relationship up front.

My grandmother was born in Czechoslovakia and came to the United States when she was only six years old. On her first day of school in Oklahoma, she came home early in tears. She told her parents that the teacher didn't understand her. Her father told her, "It is not your teacher's responsibility to understand you. It is *your* responsibility to understand your teacher." With that he turned her around, she got back on her pony, and went back to school determined to become an effective communicator.

Special note: The ability to speak Spanish is a valuable skill to learn, especially in the United States, because it will enhance your business opportunities as we move forward. The percentage of Spanish-speaking people in our population is increasing and will continue to do so. As important as speaking English will be for them, there will still be many who will not be able to. You may be presented with better business opportunities if you can speak Spanish. In addition to this, learning Mandarin Chinese, Russian, Japanese, and German may also increase your marketability in the business world.

Be sure to educate yourself on what languages you should master in order to reach your highest potential for success in your chosen field.

Be Organized

We all have busy lives that are only getting busier. Find a way to stay organized. My best suggestion is to invest in a day planner (paper or electronic) and to meticulously keep track of key dates, deadlines, and to-do items. You must compartmentalize what needs to be done and when it needs to be done in order to stay on schedule. If you worry about everything at the same time, you will become overwhelmed and will be more likely to lose track of the urgency of certain tasks.

Don't let the "black cloud of things to do" hang over your head.

Go to Class (and Meetings)

This piece of advice is perhaps the easiest to implement in this entire book. Teachers and managers always share information during a class or meeting that is not reflected in notes, agendas, or memos. Sure, attending meetings or sitting through a lecture may be a little boring, but topics that are important to your teacher or boss will be emphasized in both verbal and nonverbal ways at these gatherings. The topics covered will undoubtedly make an impression on you and you will be more likely to remember the information in the future if you come prepared to listen and even to take notes. By paying attention, you will automatically do better on your tests and job evaluations.

Be Well Rounded

There is a tremendous focus on getting good grades in school and being a good technician at work. The way to differentiate yourself for a job or as you are applying to an educational institution is by being well rounded. Employers and universities are looking for people who give back to their community and who are natural leaders. These traits can be demonstrated by volunteering for charities that you believe strongly in. You can also become involved in various other activities in leadership roles to show your potential to lead others.

Take Care of Business, Then Have Fun

Since only you truly know the tasks you must accomplish, be sure to take care of your priorities first before lending a hand to help others or before going out to have fun.

This reminds me of my senior year in college. Interviews for college students with public accounting firms occurred during the fall semester. These on-campus functions, interviews, and out-of-town office visits took up a large chunk of my time. My friends would often say to me, "Relax, it's your senior year. You should be having fun." But my hard work paid off and I accepted my offer with Price Waterhouse in December. After that decision was firmly set, I was able to enjoy my final semester of college while many of my friends began to experience increased anxiety and worry about their post-college plans. My buckling down and doing the hard work first allowed me to have more fun that final semester.

Run, Don't Just Walk, Away from a Bad Relationship

Whether you are a teenager, young adult, divorcee, or newly married, learn as early as you can to avoid one of life's most toxic bad decisions—holding on to a bad relationship. If you are in a bad dating situation, get out as soon as possible. Relationships involve a great deal of intimacy and self-disclosure; therefore, if you are in a destructive or negative relationship, you will find yourself more vulnerable and may suffer more severe consequences the longer you remain with that person. If you become emotionally (and physically) involved with another person, you are opening up a part of you that could be hurt down the road—especially if the person you are connected to is destructive. Be mindful of this as you choose the people you want to have relationships with.

Bad dating relationships can also prevent you from meeting the *right* person. In addition, they can lead to bad marriages. Once children are involved, these bad relationships become permanent. Children do *not* make relationships better; in fact, they unknowingly exploit every weakness in a relationship.

It is easy to become hung up on your early relationships, but it is essential that you keep in mind how much you will change as you advance through college and into the real world. Once you are established in your career, you will also undergo changes as you are promoted or relocate to other branches. It is the case that few financially successful people are married to their high school sweethearts (though there are always the exceptions).

Of the people I surveyed, half of them were married to someone they met in college and the other half met their spouse through their career or just generally out in the working world. While early relationships (most of those that begin in high school) help us to establish our understanding of intimately interacting with another human being—and in many cases teach what we want or don't want out of future relationships—as you grow older, the people you become involved with will most likely be more closely aligned with you in their future goals, and you may find you have more in common with them.

Don't Let Your Pride Get You in Trouble

Have you ever been criticized harshly or had your feelings hurt? Of course you have. And it is going to happen again, guaranteed! There are going to be plenty of situations at work, in your relationships with a neighbor, partner, or family member, or in society when you are not going to have a positive interaction. Too many people take personal offense to these situations because their pride may be hurt and they accuse the other person of "disrespecting" them. The ironic part is that usually they have not previously *earned* the respect of others. Respect is earned, not given. There are also many negative people with low self-esteem out there who are looking to drag as many people as possible down to their level.

Always work toward earning the respect of your peers. There will always be people who do not give you the proper respect you deserve. It is not likely that you will be able to change them, so walk away and get over it.

When I was in my early twenties and lived in Morristown, New Jersey, I had a roommate who shared this valuable insight with me when it comes to dealing with others: The best way to handle this type of situation is to *ignore* the offending party. Many people spend far too much time feeling hatred toward others. The problem is that when you hate someone, that person holds tremendous power over you by affecting your mood at will. Hate and the combustible reaction it can perpetuate have gotten many people into trouble. You should never give someone else this power. The only exception to this is dealing with a difficult boss. In that case, you need to either find some common ground or you will need to look for a new job to maximize your long-term happiness.

Why Is Common Sense Not So Common?

One of the most important traits you need in order to be successful in life is to possess common sense. I am surprised at how many people lack this trait. If you don't believe me, just read the newspaper or watch the news—these outlets are full of stories about people who do stupid things and make common sense mistakes.

A good indicator of whether you have common sense is if you are good at basic math or not. I consider it a crime that many schools tolerate poor math skills to persist in their students. That tolerance is putting those students at a disadvantage for the rest of their lives.

The problem with people who lack common sense is that they do not have enough sense to admit that fact. I would like to offer the following bumper sticker on my website:

If it is called *common sense*, shouldn't more people have it?

10 Laws of Common Sense

We believe our ten laws of common sense could change the world:

1. Don't join a wacky cult.
2. Don't worship materialistic items.
3. Don't swear.
4. Relax, reflect, and show appreciation at least one day a week.
5. Respect your mom and dad.

6. Don't kill.
7. Avoid sexual relations outside of marriage.
8. Don't steal anything.
9. Don't lie.
10. Don't try to keep up with the Joneses.

Do you recognize them? They are, in effect, the Ten Commandments and even if you are not a religious person, these "laws" are still important to live by.

If You Are Overweight, It Is Because You Eat Too Much

Diabetes, heart disease, stroke, cancer, and a variety of other health issues have been proven to be directly linked to obesity. It seems like that evidence should be enough to motivate people to stay healthy and at a reasonable weight. Nevertheless, according to Bill Hendrick of WebMD Health News, 63.1 percent of Americans are not deterred by the health issues associated with being overweight. Therefore, I will give those folks a few more reasons to try to change their eating and exercise habits: Weight issues can lead to insecurities that will affect children for the rest of their lives. In adulthood, your weight can affect you not only socially but also professionally. Yes, it can actually affect how much money you make!

Though I am not a health or diet expert, I do know that if you feel as though you are overweight, you can do something about it. Weight, for the most part, is a simple formula calculated as the number of calories you take in versus the amount of calories you expend.

If you are overweight, you should write down everything you eat in a week (be honest) and how much exercise you have. Then compare this to a thin friend of yours. I guarantee your friend ate less and/or exercised more. There are no magical diets in which you can eat a lot and still lose weight—that's just a fact. If we all monitor our weight better, people who truly have genetic reasons that cause weight gain can be treated with the proper respect they deserve.

Also, keep an eye on your portion sizes as well. If your natural weight is around 120 pounds, you should not be eating the same portion size as someone who weighs 180 pounds. Your sex can also affect your metabolism rate. Also, you should never feel like you have to finish everything on your plate, nor should you pressure others (particularly children) to do the same.

Tattoos Are Permanent Reminders of How Stupid You Were at One Point in Your Life

A few pages back, we told you that important decisions are those with long-term consequences. This brings us to a particularly "painful" topic.

Imagine graduating from that prestigious college with a 3.9 GPA (and $100,000 of student loans). You have been asked to interview with a fantastic company that is thrilled with your résumé. You set up an interview, research the company, buy a special suit, and await the big day to come. You have trouble sleeping the night before, but that is okay because your adrenaline has kicked in. You enter the front lobby of the company and the receptionist shows you where to go and notifies the interviewer that you have arrived. Everything is running smoothly.

You then meet the interviewer in person and your interview lasts thirty exceptionally uncomfortable minutes. You cannot figure out what happened to make it such a bust on the car ride home. When you get home, you walk into your bathroom and look at yourself in the mirror. You still can't figure it out. Well let me help you. It is the tattoo that is crawling up your neck, out from your sleeves, or below your skirt.

Of course tattoos look all right and sometimes even "cool" when you are out at a nightclub, but when you are in a business setting they are very limiting, to say the least. In addition, when you are forty years old (and only half of the way to your grave), your tattoos are going to start looking horrible. Before you make the decision to get a tattoo, you should ask this question, "Will this tattoo convey the message I want to send everyone for the rest of my life?" I assure you that the answer is a resounding no.

If you want to be rebellious and get a reaction from your parents, do something that is reversible, like dying your hair purple or piercing some strange part of your body. Or at the very least, put the tattoo in a spot where even a bathing suit will hide it. You have to realize that you will go through phases in your life and adjust the permanent decisions you'll be making to fit within the right context.

Gamble for Entertainment, Not Employment

Gamble only what you can afford to lose. Although gambling seems like a lot of fun and an easy way to make a lot of money, it is not! As a profession, gambling is one of the highest stress and loneliest jobs you can have. Do not fool yourself into thinking you will make your fortune at the poker table.

Societal Factors

Society does not conform to the individual. The individual must change and adapt to society. There is a penalty for making bad decisions and showing an unwillingness to adapt. If you are not willing to adapt, you will be frustrated for the remainder of your life. Below are elements that exist in our society and global culture that need to be acknowledged in order for you to maximize your success and happiness.

Change Is Inevitable

There is *no* way not to change over the course of your lifetime. Change is a fact, even though many people want to stay the same. When you stay in one place you allow others to catch you and you risk falling farther behind your peer group. This can be an intimidating feeling when you believe you have no control over the changes happening around you. In reality, you can have a lot of control if you embrace the fact that change will occur and that it is not the end of the world. You can then use change to affect everything you don't like about your situation.

We Live in a Global Economy

Isolationism is simply not an option. One of the surprising aftereffects of 9-11, combined with the impact of the Internet and media, is that it made the world feel like a smaller place. We are now aware of what is happening all over the globe just as if it is happening in the town next to us. Now that we are aware of what is happening around the world, it is important to understand the impact this has on us in the United States:

- Freedom of the press does not mean the media is impartial. The media sensationalizes the news because they are a business that must sell advertising. Advertising is based on ratings. People do not tune in to the news if the anchor comes on and says, "Nothing really happened today so you can go back to your family and enjoy the evening." In addition, networks often have a vested political interest in what they show. We have freedom of the press, but that does not mean the press is unbiased.
- Low-end manufacturing will be sent to countries where labor is less expensive. The expected wages of Americans (and minimum wage laws) do not allow us to manufacture products domestically that are price competitive in the global market. Not only is this a non-controllable factor (which means we would waste time and energy trying to change it), but it is also not in our best interest as a country.
- Other countries that have higher employment rates and better education levels see their wages increase. As their employment rates and wages go up, they will be able to afford more convenience products and services versus focusing entirely on necessities, like food and shelter.
- As less developed countries purchase more convenience products and services, they will purchase more from the United States.
- As they purchase more from the United States, we will be able to provide more and better-paying jobs.

This will benefit you if you have the education or trade skills to handle these new and better job opportunities. Education is the single best way to improve your potential for financial success.

We Live in an Advanced Society

There are many benefits in our society today that did not exist a century ago, including care for the elderly, health care advancements, and social welfare. Unfortunately, no great strides come without a price. Our society is becoming more complex each day. The most significant price we pay today is that of education. A college degree today is what a high school degree was half a century ago. The people who do not have an adequate education or skills will fall farther and farther behind.

Many more people are getting advanced degrees beyond a four-year college degree than ever before, and this trend will continue. One of the largest problems that our society faces today is the "education gap." This gap will grow wider as some people continue not to earn their high school degrees while more and more achieve post-graduate degrees.

You must help provide for your children's education or they will be at a permanent disadvantage for the rest of their lives.

We Live in the Greatest Country in the World

Do we have some problems in this country? Yes. Are some countries great places to go on vacation? Yes. Do we *live* in the greatest country in the world? Absolutely! Do you want proof of this claim? Here is a simple calculation to rank all countries and their "greatness" in the world:

(# risking death to enter) - (# risking death to leave) = "Greatest" Factor

I guarantee the United States is #1 by a large margin.

It is very important to travel so that you can understand and respect different perspectives and cultures. Unfortunately, many people confuse a country that is beautiful and rich with historical significance with one that is better to live in. Even though we have some problems in this country, there is no better place to *live* in the world when you consider factors such as:

- Employment opportunities
- Quality of life
- Ability to own a home
- Discrimination (there is actually more in most other countries)
- Women's rights and opportunities
- Taxes (most people in other developed countries pay a higher rate)
- Health care system
- Freedom of speech

It is true the Americans, in particular, are frustrated with the way our government works and the problems we face as a nation. If we, as a country, focus on the process to solve our problems, however, we will be able to come to good solutions. And the same is true in your personal life as well.

Politically Correct and Our "No Fault" Society

Political correctness has been a cultural evolution over the last few decades so that people of all races, religions, nationalities, and sexes can be treated equally in our society. This was an essential evolution that our society needed to undergo and it was supported and mandated by many new laws and regulations. That being said, political correctness has gone too far. In many cases, it has caused negative behaviors to go uncorrected.

When analyzing your behavior, be brutally honest with yourself and accept responsibility. You must understand what you are and are not capable of. This book is cross-cultural and provides a standard equation that applies to all citizens.

Here is my logic as to why the politically correctness and the "no fault" society have gone too far:

1. Laws are in place to prevent discrimination and encourage equality of opportunity.
2. We should thank our parents for bringing us into this world and we should be happy with what they have given us. We should not blame them for what we do not have and we certainly do not have the basis to blame our entire society. Many successful people use what they do not have as fuel for their hard work, which later enables them to achieve great things.
3. Once we become teenagers, we start making the most of our own decisions. If we make good decisions, we will end up in a good place. If we make bad decisions, we will end up in a bad place. Therefore, where we end up is based on the personal choices each of us makes at a rather early age.
4. We all project a stereotype. These stereotypes can be positive or negative and are based on what we look like, our sex, the way we dress, and how we act. We also stereotype each person with whom we interact. This is usually based on our past experiences, and we tend to act based on these constructed beliefs in our interactions with other people.
5. Stereotypes are proven correct or incorrect one interaction at a time. If a person proves a negative stereotype correct, that is their fault and they need to change. If someone is in a group that has a negative stereotype and some of their peers are proving that negative stereotype to be true, that individual needs to encourage his or her peers to change their behavior instead of tolerating it.

Change must come from within, and we must accept responsibility for our actions.

The "Trophy Generation"

The current generation that is graduating from school and entering the real world over the next few years intrigues me. This is a generation that, when playing sports or participating in an activity, was always awarded a trophy, no matter whether they or their team was the winner or loser. While this certainly may help to boost children's self-esteem, it also creates a false environment in which no one feels inferior or behind another. It sounds great—almost like a perfect world—but the reality is that people who get a false sense of security in this "equal" world may become overwhelmed and even shocked by the real world they will enter.

People who work hard and excel at something they are good at will be rewarded. People who don't work hard or who stay in a field where their natural talents are below the level of others will fall behind and will not be rewarded. It sounds cruel and harsh but it is true. People who understand this fact will set more reasonable expectations for themselves and for others and will be less likely to feel completely defeated if they are not rewarded in some way for a job only adequately done.

Summary

This chapter has a lot to consider and even more to digest. You may find that after reading this you will need to change more than your peers, and change is not easy. We should remember to take each day and make it a little better than the day before. If you continue this pattern, you will eventually establish a solid foundation for your "self" that will support the remaining core elements of life.

Now that you understand how to build a solid foundation, it is time to learn more about the other mandatory core element of life— career. Most of us will spend more time at work than anywhere else, except for when we sleep. As long as you are spending that much time at your job, why not get the most out of your career? A solid career will help you fuel the highest level of success and happiness possible.

CHAPTER 7:
CAREER

As long as you have to work, why not get the most out of it? It amazes me that so many people wake up, get ready for work, work all day, then go home only to do it all over again the next day, all without thinking about their career in any strategic way. You will spend at least one-quarter of your time for over four decades doing this same routine; that is over 80,000 hours! This chapter will be the biggest differentiator for you because by maximizing the time you spend at work, you will increase your overall effectiveness in your position and will thus be able to afford more in all aspects of your life. In this chapter you will learn:

- The most valuable skills for an employee to possess
- How your skills will need to change throughout your career

- How to advance your career
- How to become an effective manager
- How to start your own business

By acquiring the skills employers demand and knowing what employers value, you will find a job or change to a better one. You may experience a time in your life when you take a break from your work—this should be a choice, not a forced decision. Here is what so many people fail to understand: When you think about your job and career, you need to think about how it fits into your relationships, family, personal goals, and financial needs—and not just for a few years, but over the course of a lifetime. Of course you cannot predict what will happen in the course of your life, but you can increase the chances of success and happiness by considering the risks and rewards each choice is likely to present to you.

If you want to become a surgeon, you should know that you will not be an established professional with a significant income until you reach your early or mid thirties. If you want to become a literature professor, you should know roughly how many job openings will be available over the next few years and how many of those lead to tenured positions. You will need to learn how to balance your strengths and interests with the market for those skills, whatever they may be. It is essential that you pick a career that will pay you enough to cover your desired lifestyle and provide you with enough financial stability.

In this chapter, we'll unveil the skills the best managers have—skills that empower them to achieve their goals and dreams. We'll also demonstrate the importance of shaping and understanding the life cycle of your career. The stages are as follows:

- Twenties—For many of you, this will be the most aggressive time in your career. Those who start the fastest will be farthest ahead in the long run. During this period you will also have the fewest distractions, such as having a spouse, owning a home, and raising children, which means you will have the most time to dedicate to your career.

- Thirties—At this point, you are likely still aggressive but you start having other demands on your time such as being married, owning a home, and having children.
- Forties—While likely still aggressive, you are tempted to take a shot at the big home run in your early forties. Your family situation is a little more stable and you feel like you are running out of time to make the big "dream" paycheck.
- Fifties—You are settled into where you are in life. You may have one more promotion ahead of you but time is running out. You also realize there is much more to life than your career. These other interests make it difficult to dedicate the necessary time to your job to earn additional promotions. Thoughts of retirement are weighing heavy on your mind. Are you financially prepared for it?
- Sixties—You always said you would retire by now but many people are not in the financial position to do so. Also, your "hobby" for the last forty years has been your career, so it may feel a little difficult to let that go.

General Advice and Observations

One evening, when I was fourteen, I remember sitting at the dinner table with my family. My father had just returned from another "half day" at work. He left by seven o'clock in the morning and returned at seven o'clock at night. He often worked in his study after dinner and also on weekends. Needless to say, he worked many more hours than the typical forty-hour work week.

My dad always had an interesting story of what he did at work on any given day and he always had so much passion about his job when he spoke of it. With his passion and all the time he spent at work, I figured he must love his job, because I certainly did not want to spend this much time at school! At dinner that particular night, I decided to ask him, "How much of your job do you enjoy?" I figured it must be well over 90 percent, which was why I was shocked when I heard him say, "Less than 50 percent." How could this man who I respect so much and who spoke so passionately about his job enjoy his work less than 50 percent? I learned early in my career that even though your job is important—and you must try to enjoy it—you will not be satisfied with your career 100 percent of the time, and that is completely natural. I believe that many people do not understand this fact as they leave the cloistered environment of school and enter the real world.

Below are highlighted areas where I have witnessed many people making common mistakes in their careers. I have included observations from my own experience that I believe will help you advance your career and increase your overall earnings without making too many mistakes along the way.

Profitability, Profitability, and Profitability

Let's start from the top. If you can determine why an organization was formed, you will more easily fit in and know how to excel. Was Exxon-Mobil started in order to find oil and refine it into gasoline? Was Boeing established to build airplanes? Was Ford created to make cars? Why are companies in business? In a nutshell, corporations are founded because they believe they can provide valuable expertise and resources to the general public—and make a profit from doing so. They attracted investors who supported the founders' ideas and believed they could generate a profit that was higher than what could be generated elsewhere. Expectation of profit is what drives investment and growth.

Why are some businesses like Exxon-Mobil still thriving while other businesses, such as Sears and General Motors—once titans in American business—are struggling to stay alive? One word: profit. If a company is profitable, it will survive. If a business is not profitable, it will go under. It is that simple. Nothing is more important than the profitability of your employer. If your employer's business is not profitable, get ready for many changes that you will not like—a pink slip may be looming on the horizon. Because your job is never "safe," you need to be thinking about these two things each day:

- How do I increase revenues?
- How do I decrease expenses?

The buck does not stop with the CEO or president of your company either. The president or CEO has to report to a board of directors, the banks, and any investors. In reality, there are very few people who do not have someone above them to whom they have to report. Work to make your boss's job easier and you will hopefully see some rewards in the workplace.

Are profits important to a charitable or government organization? Not necessarily, but there is one huge exception. When revenues do not cover the operating expenses, losses cannot be tolerated. At this point, management will make decisions that are very similar to for-profit corporations: they will either increase revenue or decrease expenses.

Work Is a Game . . . Know the Rules and Wear the Uniform

It never ceases to amaze me how people miss the real point of work—you are there to complete tasks that someone else at your company does not have time to do themselves. With that in mind, here a few tips for doing well in your workplace:

- Take on responsibility and have pride in what you do.
- Be a good team player and help others when they need it.
- Blend into the environment.
- Dress slightly neater and more professionally than the average.
- If you want to make a social statement, do it after work and away from the office.

Start Working Early

I started working when I was thirteen years old as a caddie at a local golf course. During my teenage years, I also worked as a busboy, cook, host, and bartender's assistant at a restaurant. Most memorably, during a summer break in college, when I was nineteen, I had a job with a construction company. I was responsible for doing everything that no one else wanted to do, like running errands, cleaning, and digging ditches. Toward the end of the summer my boss—one of the owners—asked me to dig a trench along the seawall he had at his house that was about 80 yards long. As I neared the end he asked me, "Do you know why you are digging that trench?" I said, "Of course; the soil is sliding under the dock and the water is not deep enough for your boat." My boss laughed and said, "That isn't it. I want to make sure you are going back to college." I replied, "You don't have to worry about that a bit." I already knew I was going to college to advance my opportunities beyond digging a ditch.

My experience taught me what the options were if I did not obtain my high school or college degrees. After majoring in accounting, I must admit that the pay was much better than in construction and I enjoyed working in an air-conditioned office.

There are many, many career options out there, but you need to work hard for the attractive ones because there is also a lot of competition in the world. Opportunities go to those who seek them out.

Salaries Are Based on Supply and Demand, Not Relative Importance

Compensation is about being rewarded for providing a skill that employers need and are willing to pay for. People get paid more by developing a skill that is needed, that few others have, and that will turn into profitable products and services that can be successfully sold in the marketplace. Many people believe the compensation they receive for a job should be measured by the relative importance of that job. While this may be true in theory, jobs that we may consider very important—teachers, police officers, firefighters, et al—can be performed by a larger number of people in society. Thus, the high supply for these types of jobs drives the salaries down.

Another example comes from the time I spent working in the professional sports arena. It was amazing how many people were willing to be underpaid for the opportunity to work in such a profession. The reason is that for every open job, professional sports managers receive hundreds of applications. This is the ultimate example of high supply driving down salaries. People are willing to work for almost half of what they could make elsewhere and so they are paid less for their work.

It is important to develop a valuable skill that someone is willing to pay adequately for.

Being Respected Is More Important than Being Liked

This is one of the most difficult adjustments to make when you enter the workforce because, in school, popularity is based on being liked. At work, you need to be respected for your skill set. This requires you to be fair and do what is best for the company. Sometimes, these decisions will not be popular. Good decisions will help you tremendously as you continue your career.

You need to learn to do the right thing and lead by example. Saying the right thing is the first step toward doing the right thing . . . but it is not the same in the end.

Consistently Expand and Improve Your Network

If you want to remain at the front of your field, if you want to maintain your success by building on it, and if you want to become one of those individuals who get the opportunities and promotions, it is absolutely and positively essential that you build your personal network inside and outside of your company. Without a network, people in professional careers stagnate. The wider and better your network is, the better you are able to complete assigned tasks. Also, a strong network is usually a good sign that someone will be a good manager. A few tips for building a network include:

- Join industry-specific networking groups.
- Return to school for advanced education.
- Volunteer to be on the board of directors for a charitable organization.
- Help anyone who seeks your assistance in finding a job to the extent it is possible.
- Meet with professional recruiters ("headhunters").

In terms of attending company functions, many times these events provide alcohol for the attendees. While some believe that you should not drink at company functions, this is not necessarily true. Oftentimes, the best way to get to know someone is by having a few drinks with them. Be careful, however, that you do not overdo it and become completely inebriated. If you are going to meet with the CEO of the company after the function, don't drink so you can be on the top of your game. Also, if you are someone who has difficulty moderating how much you drink, steer clear of the alcoholic beverages at these professional events and stick to soda or water.

Know Who Your Customer Is

Many employees who are not in sales believe that they do not have any customers; however, this is a misconception, because everyone has customers. The reason you have a job is because someone needs something done and they are willing to pay you to do it. If you do not keep them happy by providing good customer service, these people will find someone who will and you will be out of a job.

For example, when I was in accounting and finance, my customers were mostly inside the company. They were other department heads who relied on me and my department to collect cash, pay bills, and provide financial information for them to properly manage their department.

Everyone needs to make sure their customers are well taken care of . . . or someone else will.

Identify Efficiencies

In today's economic environment, it is the fast that devour the slow (not the big that swallow the small as in times past). Therefore, efficiency is an important trait to possess. Those who can get the most done in the least amount of time are typically considered the most valuable.

Many people become comfortable in the tasks they perform because they have always done those tasks a particular way. Unfortunately, our society is not the same as it was fifty years, ten years, or even just one year ago. As a successful business professional, you must learn to adapt the way you perform your job, especially if it increases your efficiency in the workplace. The way to do this is to:

- Understand the flow of the overall process.
- Identify the purpose and who relies on the product of the overall process.
- Prioritize each task in the process.
- Look for the duplication of tasks in that process.
- Identify technological solutions for tasks that are performed manually.

Challenge the Need to Perform Tasks

When you are assigned a task, you should say to yourself, "Why is this task important?" If you don't understand why the task is important, one of two situations will occur:

1. If you are right and the task is not important, you saved time.
2. If you are wrong and it is essential to perform the task, your boss will help you understand why that task is important. That is an important growth opportunity and will make you a better contributor to the team in the future.

Think like an owner. If you owned this business, would you want people doing unnecessary and inefficient tasks?

Maintain a Clean Desk (versus a Messy One)

It is true that we can point to folks with messy desks who are successful and productive. And we can point to folks with clean desks who struggle with productivity and meeting their work requirements. However, my experience and judgment after working in organizations with highly productive professionals for over twenty years is this: The additional effort you invest in keeping your personal workspace organized, neat, and presentable will reduce your time stress and force you to manage the paper that comes across your desk in a timely fashion. Business involves reading and processing paperwork and documents; that is the reality of it. A messy desk piled with documents means one thing: Those reports, spreadsheets, PowerPoints, or proposals collecting on your desk have not been read and managed by you. All too often, you'll run into a bad result. The paper you needed to read or react to for your boss, an important client, or colleague will be buried under another report you have not yet managed. You'll be embarrassed. You'll have a left a poor impression. And you may risk repercussion from your higher-ups for failing to be prepared.

My question is, "If you are not organized, how can you be efficient?" If your desk is messy at the end of the day, clean it up. If you are too busy to read or process the daily flow of critical papers, set up a system to establish priorities and communicate across, up, and down the chain of command about timetables. This process will ensure that you do not forget anything and it will set you up the next day to have a productive shift. There are plenty of books on managing your activities. Find one, read it, and follow its instructions.

Do It Right the First Time

It is important that we all understand another reality about business: In the business world, executives and decision makers focus intensely on efficiency and productivity. Many books, conferences, papers, meetings, and speeches have made various cases for the importance of innovation and creativity in most areas of private enterprise. But no business will succeed if it is has poor productivity and efficiency over a sustained period of time. Innovation will fail without well-managed systems. Your bosses or future bosses will reward individuals who produce more quality work during the same period of time as other individuals. Productivity means profits. Productivity means goals are met. Productivity is execution. But productivity does not mean you sacrifice accuracy for speed. The most important part of your job is to be accurate. An error can cause more work for not only you, but for all the people who rely on the work you produce to efficiently do their jobs. If you process information a little slower than some, take the time to be accurate. If you are falling behind, you may need to add more hours to your workweek. You will enjoy your free time, family, relationships, and personal time if you have done your work accurately, to high standards, and on time.

Never Say "It's Not My Job"

When your boss or coworker asks you to do something, there are three possible answers: "yes," "sure," or "no problem." If something needs to be done, someone needs to do it. You will earn a high level of respect if you are the type who always goes above and beyond your job description. People who get raises and are promoted are the ones who consistently perform tasks that are outside their current job description.

Just get it done!

Warning: Don't become a pushover, though. When you take on additional tasks, be sure you are selecting high-profile, valuable work. When you take on more work, use it as an opportunity to delegate the more menial tasks. If you become the pushover, everyone will dump unwanted tasks on you and you will become miserable.

The Only Constant Is Change

When I was a chief financial officer, one of my favorite people in my department was an accounts payable clerk who was conscientious, honest, and a team player. When we decided to upgrade our system as part of a broad initiative to improve accounting efficiency, she was confronted with many changes to her job. She always had a positive attitude at work. However, one day she came to me and said that she just couldn't handle the pace of changes. She felt overwhelmed. At this point I knew we were changing too fast, but I also knew that we could not stop. As we talked, I realized that she did not always understand why we were changing our system. We talked about our objectives in more detail. I also asked her if there were parts of her job that she would like to change, and she said there were several.

At that point I realized this: there will always be change but it comes in two forms: change you control and change you don't. Always take control over change if you can. Always understand why change is occurring and how you would like the various change(s) to benefit you. If you don't do this, change will continue and it will lead to great frustration and possible burnout.

When she understood more about the function of our changing systems, she suggested additional changes that accentuated her strengths. In addition to becoming more efficient and productive, she also enjoyed her job more than ever because she knew that everything she was doing was important.

Identifying Problems Is the Easy Part

Identifying problems is the easy part; the hard part is developing and implementing the solutions. Most change and efficiency initiatives fail due to poor cost justification, inadequate planning, or lack of consensus building among those affected by the initiative. The steps for the successful implementation of change must include:

- Educating yourself on the options (technological options can be particularly complicated to assess)
- Developing a clear plan and timeline
- Dedicating more hours to work throughout the change period
- Building consensus with those affected by the change
- Gaining the political support from those above you to sponsor the change initiative
- Justifying any additional costs to implement the changes (payback period)
- Identifying any departments that may be affected in a negative manner and showing them why the change is important to improving the overall organization
- Minimizing turf battles for new responsibilities

Opportunities for Solution

When you encounter a problem on the job, don't tell your boss about the problem only. Suggest a proposed solution as well. This small evolution in the way you perform your job will have a profound impact in several ways. It is an opportunity to show your boss your potential. As you move up, a very important skill to possess is the ability to problem solve. You will deal with more exceptions as you move up and it is important for those above you to see how you handle these stressful situations.

The proposed solution is a learning opportunity. If there is a better solution, your boss can educate you as to what it is. Then, you will be better able to handle future situations that arise. The proposed solution will also save your boss time. It is likely that you are more familiar with the issues than your manager. If your solution makes sense, your superior will likely sign off on it quickly. The last benefit (a selfish one) is that the agreed solution will likely be most tolerable for you.

Tip: Whenever there is a mistake or problem, always let your boss hear it from you *first*. If someone else gets there before you, it could embarrass your boss and limit how he or she handles the problem, and the trust he or she places in you may be lost.

Go Upstream to Fix Problems

When presented with a problem, you must first understand the root cause. A problem can be fixed but it does not prevent future problems. The first step is to identify whether this is a recurring or nonrecurring problem. For all recurring problems, you must fix the root cause or it will happen again.

For example, assume a salesperson always writes up a sale incorrectly. When this is recorded by Accounting, it could lead to inaccurate information and the collection of the wrong amount of money. This problem could easily be fixed by the accountant each time, yet this problem will occur again the next time a sale is made by this particular salesperson. The solution is to educate the salesperson or set context as to the importance of the way he records his sales. This will prevent the problem from occurring again.

As you can see from this example, the best approach to solving a recurring problem is to educate or set context for a colleague upstream on any given process so that they understand how someone downstream relies on what they do and they realize the importance of maintaining accuracy.

Internal versus External Motivation

You will always have motivation in your life. The more you can motivate yourself internally, the more you and your boss will be happy with your performance. If you do not have internal motivation, then your boss will have to apply external motivation—which is a less ideal situation for both of you. And if that doesn't work, the next step is that you will be looking for another job.

What Have You Done for Me Lately?

Too many employees rely on previous quality of work to justify raises and promotions in the future. You need to prove yourself anew each and every day. Perform above your job expectations every day and you will be sure to see the rewards of your hard work and motivation.

In God We Trust, All Others Bring Data

When I was with Price Waterhouse, my largest client, Exxon, was the best-run company I had ever seen, and they had the highest respect for the finance and accounting departments. A common saying that I heard was "In God we trust, all others bring data." I was amused by this saying when I first heard it. Several years later, and with a lot more experience, I finally understood what it meant. Too many people execute on initiatives before they are adequately contemplated.

When I was with the Texas Rangers, I used this philosophy for anyone who wanted to vary from the established budget. I required that the department head submit written documentation supporting their proposal. As people went through the process of documenting what they wanted to do, it forced them to document the raw data.

If cost justification didn't work on paper, then they wouldn't waste anyone's time trying to push through a bad idea.

Most People Overestimate Their Value, Do You?

What is your value to your company? How replaceable are you? Most people do not want to acknowledge the true answers to these questions. Fact of the matter is that it is likely that you are easily replaceable.

I call this the "locker room effect." People are always amazed at how professional athletes can complain about making millions of dollars. The reason is because their world consists of the other twenty-four guys sitting in the locker room. If someone else is making more but batting and fielding worse, it is only natural to make the assumption they are being underpaid.

The same kind of thinking occurs in business, and in this case, the "locker room" becomes other people at your level or in your department. These groups form and then pieces of information are exchanged. This can lead to a negative cycle of thinking that those around you are being compensated higher for their work. As doubts creep in, your dissatisfaction level increases, you may develop a poor attitude, and become a distraction to your coworkers. This negative cycle could lead to your quitting or being asked to leave.

The key is to work hard and make life easier for your boss—that should be your number one priority at your job. Work every day like your job is at risk and you will find that it never will be.

Search for Win-Win Situations

When you played games as a child, your focus was on winning. You always knew that you won when you correctly identified the loser. In your career, winning does matter, because few folks want to associate with those who regularly lose. That is another reality of business. You want the people you work with, sell to, or service to feel like they won as well. The reason this is so important is because when you win, you will take a step forward. If the person you were dealing with is perceived as the loser, he will take a step back. Then he will feel that he needs to beat you on the next interaction in order for you to come back to his level. This means that you will have a big red target on your forehead and your "opponent" will get you back at some point.

Sales Is Great Except for One Thing . . . the Rejection

Many people look at salespeople and think they have the easiest job in the company because they are always in a good mood. If a salesperson is selling then, yes, her job *is* great and a lot of fun. What many people don't understand, though, is that it is extremely important for a salesperson to have a positive attitude at all times because they face a tremendous amount of failure and rejection on a regular basis. They are constantly put in situations where the absolute best salesperson is successful about 20 percent of the time (most are successful less than 10 percent of the time). How would you like your job if you were right only one-fifth of the time?

The main challenge a salesperson can face is if she believe sales is about talking and telling the best jokes—but it's not. It is about listening to a customer's needs, understanding those needs, and then providing a solution. If you truly want to earn the trust of a client, provide a solution to a problem that does not involve your company. That will prove to your client that you have their best interests in mind and not just your bottom line.

As for everyone else in a company, if the salespeople don't sell, you could soon be out of a job. Sales are the lifeblood of a company. Everyone must do as much as they can to increase revenue. If you do not increase revenue, then your company will be forced to cut expenses. Cutting expenses is extremely painful for everyone.

Another interesting fact about sales is that it is surprisingly unstable considering it is the lifeblood of a company. The main cause of this instability is the constant struggle between salespeople and management. Management is regularly tweaking the compensation structure so that salespeople remain aggressive and that they do not make too much money. This often leads to good salespeople leaving and joining a competitor where there is a perception of more stability, less altering of the compensation structure, and an ability to make more money. When customers follow a departed salesperson it is detrimental to everyone left at the company.

Acquiring versus Acquired

Acquisitions are a common fact of business life that is here to stay. These can work in your favor by providing you with additional opportunities or to your detriment if they are looking to identify efficiencies. During the transition period following an acquisition, it is very important that you know your role.

If you are *acquiring* another company, make sure you are doing the job to the best of your abilities. Also ensure that you have the ability to handle the additional responsibilities that will come your way. This scenario is the more secure of the two, but remember to never put yourself in a situation where someone could use the acquisition as an excuse to get rid of you. Vernon experienced five acquisitions in ten years in financial services as the acquirer. He says to never underestimate the acquired company's people. They have smart people, too, and they are not the enemy. Treat them like the enemy at your own risk—and don't burn bridges.

If you are *being acquired* then the situation is much more complicated. The acquiring company is likely interested in your company's sales channel, products, or the technology possessed. If you are in an administrative role and there is mention of efficiencies, you are what they are talking about! In this situation, you need to work hard but also get your résumé circulated. Remember: It is much easier to find a job when you have a job. In addition, upon receiving an offer from another company, you will find out how much the acquiring company truly wants you to stay. Lastly, if you are let go, do not feel like a black sheep. This will likely happen at least once in your career.

Getting Canned—If It Hasn't Happened, It Will

Competition, acquisitions, technology, and the availability of information have made it virtually impossible for a company to stay on top in their industry for a prolonged period. Virtually every company will experience a lack of profitability, growth, or will be acquired at some point. This will force the company to make changes, often drastic. Companies will be forced to terminate a minority of the employees in order to protect the majority. This is the reason that people feel as if companies no longer pay loyalty to their employees.

This can also be used to your advantage. In times of change, you will have the best opportunities presented to you. Keeping a keen eye on the profitability of your company and responding appropriately will help you protect your position.

In case you do not know anyone who has been fired, you do now . . . me! Although the Texas Rangers were larger than the Dallas Stars, the Dallas Stars' management "won" most of the key positions—along with some people who the owner infused into the combined entity—when the front offices for both teams were brought together to form Southwest Sports Group. I was one of the few people from the Texas Rangers side who "won" when I was put in charge of the finances for both teams.

I learned a valuable lesson during this period. In addition to a job being terminated due to an error, you can also be terminated for being apart from the pack. When you find yourself in an odd-man-out situation, you have two choices: (1) get back with the crowd; or (2) start interviewing. I saw the signs, but I did not want to be honest with myself. In fact, months before I was actually fired, I told the person who made the decision to wait until October to fire me, when a couple of big initiatives would be completed. I was joking at the time but when the first week of October rolled around, I was out and their company person was in.

It was a difficult time for me, personally, but the company actually did me a favor (it just took me a while to realize that). If you are fired, do not feel embarrassed or ashamed. You will be surprised how many people you know have gone through the same situation. I was afraid to tell people but when I started to let my friends know, one friend told me not to worry because he had been fired . . . twice! I could not believe how common it was, and how supportive people were to my plight. And by letting people know I was out of job, I could start to network and ask others to put in a good word for me with their friends or companies.

There is a very supportive network out there that you only find out about when you are out of a job. This network includes recruiters, networking groups (such as the Financial Executives Networking Group), online job searching websites (such as Monster.com and CareerBuilder.com), and your personal network of friends and people you have met throughout your career.

Interview If You Are Not Being Treated Fairly

While I was with the Rangers, we decided to hire a director of purchasing. We interviewed numerous people, but it became clear that there was only one person who was right for the job. She turned out to be even better than expected. She had the perfect balance of intelligence, interpersonal skills, and business acumen. After a few years, her position was getting a little stale since she had attacked all the significant projects. This was also the time that she felt she was ready for a considerable pay increase to make her consistent with pay scales in comparable companies.

In short, she was absolutely correct and she had the data to prove it. Unfortunately, she had two factors going against her. First, professional sports do not pay well, unless you are a player. Second, she had done such a good job of putting a process in place that her skills were not as needed as they once were. My only significant advice I could offer to her was to interview for new jobs. Ultimately, she found a better opportunity but it took her about two years. She was able to be more productive on the job because her future included opportunities outside her current company, but she also found a better opportunity that helped her achieve her personal goals. Her subordinate received a promotion and a raise. The end result is that the company was in a better situation and so was she.

Many companies do not want to acknowledge this, but interviewing should be encouraged. This is what will keep employees and employers in balance in the future. Any time you feel you are not being treated or compensated fairly, you should interview. One of two situations will occur:

- You will find a better situation that will be good for you personally.
- You won't find anything better. In that case, you will better appreciate your current situation and be a more valuable employee.

Always maintain an updated version of your résumé. You will find that the more attractive your experience is to other companies, the more valuable you are to your current employer.

Following are three important interview tips:

- Watch out for the biggest sucker question in an interview: "Can you tell me about yourself?" You may be very proud of parts of your career that are irrelevant to the interviewer. You should turn this question around and say something like, "We have plenty of time to talk about my background, but I was hoping I could learn more about the position first." Upon finding out more about their needs, you can talk about your experience in a way that fits those needs. You will seem like a perfect match for the job!
- Get the job and then decide whether you want it. Many people do not actively pursue an opportunity when interviewing. They have an attitude of "I am not sure I want to work here." This attitude can turn an interviewer off quickly. Actively pursue a job with great interest. Then when you get an offer, you can ask the tough questions to make sure you want to accept the offer. The reason why an offer is so important is that it gives you the maximum amount of leverage—leverage at your existing employers because now you can go somewhere else easily and earn more money or have more responsibility. It also gives you leverage with your potential employer because the company has now made a commitment to you and they do not want to fail.
- Don't burn bridges when you do leave. Many people get so excited about their new opportunity that they do not leave their old employer properly. There will likely come a time

when you will need a reference and you want to be able to go back to a previous employer and receive stellar praise. Also, future employers will research your reputation and validate your résumé. Put your previous employer in a position to say only positive things about you.

Comfortable Employees (Swans) versus Aggressive Career Growth (Bulls)

One fact that I found most surprising when I started my career was that not everyone was like me. In fact, I found that there were different types of people and different types of jobs. As I gained more experience, I realized it was important for the type of person to match with the right type of job to maximize morale and performance. To help you understand this, I have categorized people into two broad categories; those comfortable with their positions I call "Swans" and those who are in an aggressive career growth mode I call "Bulls." After reading this section, you may recognize yourself as one or the other, or you may find you have some of both. Your age, personal situation, and the point you are in your career will have an effect on whether your inner Bull or Swan is the more dominant. The difference is generally the result of your personal situation versus your long-term goals and age. Be reassured that identifying with one or the other is nowhere near as important as applying the insights to follow to your situation and your workplace. In this section, I will explore the importance of this classification and why companies need a blend of both types.

The Fast Eat the Slow

In the 1900s, big companies ate the small companies. That started to change as technology advanced during the 1990s. The transition is fully in place and now—the fast companies eat the slow. Companies stay at the top of their industry for shorter and shorter periods of time. Reinventing a company is done every few years and no company is immune. In addition, government jobs used to be viewed as different from business, but there are fewer differences perceived now as the years go by.

Historically, people wanted to start and end their careers with the same company. Today, you will likely work for several different companies throughout your working life. Although there is very low job stability, there is greater opportunity than ever before. This has caused greater conflict for many employees. In order to function in this new environment, you must understand your role so that you can set your goals appropriately.

Life Cycle of Your Career

As mentioned at the beginning of this chapter, your age will likely be a key influence in understanding your role. You will likely be more aggressive earlier in your career because you have more time and fewer distractions, like a spouse, house, or children. As you get older, you will become more comfortable with who you are and how you want to allocate your time.

Advantages and Disadvantages of Employees Who Are Comfortable (Swans)

There are distinct advantages of employees who are comfortable with their particular roles. Swans are less susceptible to looking for a new job, thus increasing consistency. Consistency provides value in two primary ways:

- Customers enjoy a distinct benefit when dealing with a company on a consistent basis that knows and understands their needs.
- There is a high cost to turnover that manifests itself in the cost to recruit and train new employees.

Swans also pose distinct disadvantages. These employees are generally adverse to change. This can cause a company to fall behind their competition.

Some common examples of Swans are people in manufacturing or administrative roles. They can also be people in careers that do not change dramatically from one year to the next, like a teacher or police officer. Consistency and low turnover are essential in these positions in order to be most effective.

Advantages and Disadvantages of Employees Who Are Aggressive (Bulls)

The advantages of Bulls center on their willingness to go fast and do what it takes to move ahead. The main drawback of Bulls is that they need to be constantly challenged and need room to grow. Oftentimes, it is easy to keep someone challenged early in their career but as they move up, the path starts becoming a little gridlocked. This will lead to frustration for Bulls. To combat this problem, the company must create a culture that allows Bulls to consider positions outside their company so that the pipeline can remain open. This can result in a lack of loyalty to the firm if most Bulls realize they will not be at the firm for more than a few years.

Some common examples of these environments include large public accounting firms, law firms, and investment banks, where young associates put in long hours to work for many clients. This helps develop a breadth of experience for these young associates. Only a limited number of associates will be able to make partner or principal. The vast majority of associates will be "encouraged" to leave the firm. Many Bulls will also decide they do not want to dedicate as much time and energy to their job to make partner or principal, in which case they will leave the firm upon finding another opportunity.

An additional disadvantage resulting from industries full of Bulls is that clients are usually served by people who are learning on the job. Bulls will do a large bulk of the work and many will not have direct experience on a client's issues. By the end of the project, the Bull will be an expert and repositioned for other clients. This effectively means that a client is paying a firm to train their associates.

Ideally, Have a Blend and Respect Both Types

The ideal company should have a mixture of both Swans and Bulls. The Swans need to realize that they will still need to continuously change but it will not be at the same pace as the Bulls. Swans will:

- Be an important part of doing routine tasks that aggressive people normally do not want to do.
- Help provide a sense consistency for clients.
- Provide on-the-job training for Bulls who have potential but lack relevant experience.

In this environment, Bulls need to respect the role of Swans. Bulls will work more hours than Swans in most cases and be compensated differently. Bulls need to understand the importance of working hard so that they can attain the next promotion to which a Swan is not aspiring. This will require a delicate balance. An infusion of Bulls is absolutely necessary in the future because they will push a company ahead and ensure that it remains competitive.

Which One Are You?

If your company has created a culture that accepts both roles, let your boss know which one you would like to be—or which one you have to be due to your personality. Your boss can then help you set the appropriate responsibilities, goals, and expectations. If your company does not have a culture that accepts both, you will need to fit into the culture until you can find a job that is more suitable to your long-term goals and expectations. Sometimes you can adapt your job to your goals but oftentimes you cannot. If you are not happy with your current situation, you need to interview with other companies to see if there is a more appropriate role for you somewhere else.

Don't Underestimate the Power of Networking

Vernon describes himself as a "bullswan," and many of us have both tendencies depending on the situation. When Vernon was in the learning organization at Bank of America, he saw a need for the organization to maintain and improve the skills of the 700+ learning professionals. After initial attempts at funding such an idea were not successful, Vernon scheduled a meeting with an executive two levels above to pitch his idea. The executive gave the okay but also told

Vernon that he had no funding. Over the next several months, Vernon created an organization that had its own web portal, curriculum, tools, and job aids. How did he do this with no funding? He used the power of his network. Vernon reached out to a vast organization, found champions, and got various groups to donate hours each month to the "Trainer Learning Center" (TLC). The web portal, tools, and materials were all leveraged from talent throughout the organization. It's amazing what you can do when the energy of one person ignites the fire in others with a similar vision.

Advice on Advancing Your Career

Many people want the big paycheck so they can have a nice house and all the perquisites that go with being in upper management. These positives are easy to see. Unfortunately, most people don't ever see the negatives that go along with such a promotion. This section should help you think through whether you want to be promoted or not. Then, if you decide you want a promotion, you will gain valuable insight as how to go about getting it.

Do You Have the Time?

This is the first question you should ask yourself whenever embarking on a new venture or taking up a new position in your company. Virtually all promotions require more time. There are new responsibilities and requirements that you have to learn. You also need to make sure that you instill confidence in those around you that you are capable of handling the job. Early on, you will be on a very short leash until you earn trust and respect.

Your desire to pursue a promotion also needs to be a family decision if you are in a committed relationship, are married, or have children. Your spouse needs to be in full support of your decisions. In unfortunate cases, some spouses may want for you to increase the size of your paycheck but are not willing to give up the needs he or she has on your time outside of work. This time stress can be very damaging to your relationship, particularly if you have children.

Getting Promoted Can Be Overrated

Don't say you were never warned. When you get promoted, you move farther from the midpoint. You add more positives in the form of a higher salary, bonuses, and other benefits, but you will also find more negatives. The negatives of a promotion include the following:

- An increased demand on your time
- Need to be accessible on nights and weekends
- Additional out-of-town travel
- Deal with more OPPs (other people's problems) that are discussed further below
- Need to develop new skills
- Forced to make more difficult decisions
- Your success is based on the performance of others
- No longer in direct control of results
- Politics are more complicated
- More risk that you will lose your job in situations of power changes and acquisitions
- More pressure to produce results
- More difficulty finding a comparable job at the same level of compensation at another company

Earn Respect and Do the Job before You Ask for a Promotion

Many people want a promotion before they agree to do the work required of them. This is a dangerous attitude to have. If you are promoted and then you cannot perform the job properly, you will likely be fired. Taking on the added responsibilities before being promoted is a safe trial run for you. You will experience the job so you will know whether you want it and whether you can do it. If you can't do the job or you don't want the promotion, you can step back into your original role. You will usually have more support from your superiors because you will be going above and beyond your normal responsibilities (and it means they don't have to do it). This is a great way to earn respect from those in positions above yours. Keep in mind that a company can always retroactively compensate you for performing additional responsibilities on an interim basis in the form of a bonus or higher rating that affects your overall pay grade.

The Levels of Promotion

When I started my career at Price Waterhouse, I was a staff accountant and was evaluated based on my technical skills. After three years, I was promoted to senior accountant. At that point, I was evaluated on my technical skills and my ability to manage others effectively. I was surprised to find out that many accountants who were strong technically were not very good at supervising others. In hindsight, this is not a surprise. Accountants are high achievers academically and have relied on their own abilities to be better than their peers. When you supervise others, you must rely on their ability to get the job done. This is a very difficult transition for many people to make. Conversely, many people who are average technicians can become excellent supervisors. This is why some say that "C" students actually run the world.

The following lists the general requirements for different levels of work. If you do not have familiarity with these requirements, you should pursue additional education so that you can prepare yourself for these opportunities:

- Low level—You are evaluated on your technical skills and productivity.
- Mid level—You are evaluated on managing others to get required tasks done efficiently. It is more important for you to be a good manager of others rather than being the best technician.
- Upper level—You are evaluated on your ability to motivate others, negotiate and sell, increase profitability, be creative, have foresight, understand legal issues, manage financial statements, and respect the need for administrative tasks.

Find a Mentor

There are definitely easier ways of getting promotions and this is a key point. Find someone above you in the organization with whom you share common interests. For me, the common interest I sought was golf. Golf was not necessarily the coolest sport in high school but it enabled me to develop an important skill. Many people like to play golf and there is a significant amount of business done on the golf course. When rounding out a foursome, people always want to find the best golfer available. This enabled me to spend some time with people several levels above my current position. Some of these morphed into mentor relationships.

The key to developing a mentor relationship is to be coachable. This sounds easy enough but as a friend of mine once told me, most people do not have "balanced introspection." You need to receive advice objectively and create an environment where your mentor can be brutally honest. Most people enjoy helping others. When people respond and prosper from that help, it is even more enjoyable.

Respect and Understand the Red Tape

As you continue to receive promotions and move higher up the corporate ladder, you will encounter more red tape to work around and added tasks that seem to have little, if no, added value. These tasks can include managing budgets, addressing legal issues, dealing with human resources, and understanding information technology constraints. Many people focus too much on the responsibilities that they were good at prior to being promoted and stay away from new responsibilities.

You must embrace and learn about new responsibilities during the early stages of your promotion. This is when people will have the most patience in teaching you. After that, they will simply distance themselves from you and you will find yourself alone and possibly without a job.

Dallas versus Fort Worth Negotiating Styles

I am not sure there are two large cities like Dallas and Fort Worth that are so geographically close yet so different. The saying in Texas is that Dallas is where the east ends and Fort Worth is where the west begins. One of the biggest differences I noticed was when I was in sales. The negotiating styles with clients were completely different.

The Dallas style was to give a high bid and then the client lowballed you. You went back and forth with your client in classic northeastern style, beating each other up, until you finally agree on a price. The Fort Worth style was to sit down with your client and talk for about thirty to forty-five minutes. Then at the end of the meeting, you would slide the proposal across the table. The client would either say yes or no. If they said yes, you had a client for life. If they said no, they would never take your call again. It forced people to bring the fairest price to the table right at the beginning. Once I realized this difference, it made the process surprisingly comfortable and efficient.

When having business dealings, or even personal dealings, be sure to sense which is the preferred negotiating style by the opposite party. Selecting the right style will maximize your chances of success. Let's also encourage everyone to use the Fort Worth style . . . it makes life so much better!

Push versus Pull Promotions

Some people push their way into situations and some are pulled in for being good at what they do. A warning sign for me was when people were trying to push their way into a higher position. In my career, I have learned to appreciate people who aggressively pursued new tasks and projects. I was wary of people who were simply pushing for a promotion to get a bigger paycheck or trying to grow their "empire." These people are usually not team players and will be very disruptive to a department's cohesiveness and productivity.

People should concentrate on being pulled into a new role. If you want to be promoted, you should demonstrate that you have the capability to perform additional tasks along with showing that you are a team player. At a low level, you can be a high performer by yourself. However, that does not work as you move up in an organization.

When You Are Promoted, You Have a Choice

When you are promoted, you have a choice. You can either continue to do things the same way your former boss did, even if they were inefficient or even annoying. Or you can use the promotion as an opportunity to change the elements that used to annoy you. If it used to annoy you, I am sure it will continue to annoy the person who assumed your old role. Use a promotion as an opportunity to make changes for the better of everyone below you.

Where Is Your Next Promotion?

Be aware of where your next promotion could come from. Many people start the race and run as fast as they can. The smart employee will first ask where the finish line is and stroll their way over. When you know where you are headed you can better develop necessary new skills and expand your personal network to include the key influencers in the decision to promote you.

Shift areas if you need to. After a prolonged period at the same officer level in one area, Vernon shifted to another area within the company where his skills were in higher demand and more appreciated. He was promoted two officer levels in just under three years, which was half as long as he had held the lower officer position.

Budgets Must Be Tied to Operating Decisions

One of the biggest reasons that people who have just been promoted fail stems from their lack of understanding and respect for the financial function of a company. Companies are in existence to make a profit. The sooner you understand this, the better you will do in your company.

The primary way that a company controls profitability is through the use of budgets. Budgets ensure that the operating plan for the coming year will generate a reasonable profit. But budgets do not exist in a vacuum; they are the quantification of planned operating decisions. Financial results are the analysis of the financial impact as operating decisions are executed. If you change an operating decision, it will affect the financial results of your department and the company as a whole. Take the time to understand the correlation. Said another way, pretend that you are a professional golfer. The financials are your score card and the budget tells you the par for each hole. You need to understand that the decisions you make on the course can affect your score. You are in control of your performance, not the accounting department.

Below is a flowchart that shows the parallels between the operating and financial cycles of a company:

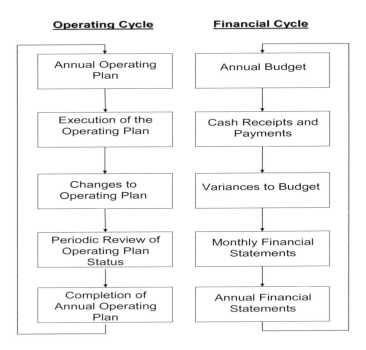

Do Women and Minorities Have an Advantage?

In our modern society, we have an obligation to help people whose life journey is considerably more difficult. This is the point of equal opportunity laws and initiatives that are in effect to help women and minorities in the workplace. This means that white males need to be better than—not just as good as—their female and minority counterparts to get a promotion. This is also a clear advantage for women and minorities that they should acknowledge and then use to their advantage. Previously, women and minorities would stay away from companies in which they were poorly represented. This is no longer the case. Those companies are now under pressure to provide a better representation of women and minorities in their upper management. This can be an excellent opportunity that should be researched and pursued by women and minorities.

Vernon comes to his views from having different experiences as an African American in the financial world. Due to the focus companies put on having a diverse workplace, the competition was always fierce to get any coveted positions. Vernon's position is that the minority candidate has to be clearly better than the non-minority candidate to get the job. This makes the job of the hiring manager much easier and clear-cut. After being in the workplace for six years, Vernon realized his situation and went back to school to get his MBA. Once attained, he felt that this point on his résumé clearly set him apart from non-minority candidates without an advance degree. Twenty years later he feels that it not only helped his banking career but his consulting careers as well.

Hopefully in the near future, we will continue to broaden these considerations to include people based on their economic status. It is important to provide opportunities to those who are less fortunate but who are capable of doing good work.

Managing Other People

Early in your career, it is important to develop technical expertise. As you demonstrate that you have mastered the technical components of any given job, it is then time to work on improving your management skills. The difficult part of managing others is realizing that your success is based on the combined work product of not only yourself but also those under you, and not how much you can do on your own. Following are some important points to keep in mind as you progress toward a managerial position.

The People Who Need the Most Help Are the Least Likely to Get It

When I was promoted to senior accountant at Price Waterhouse, the company sent me to a special training session on how to manage others. I found the course to have a lot of common sense points but it was a helpful refresher. Those who complained that the training session was a waste of time turned out to be some of the worst managers, as they could not see beyond their own obsession with using time productively to realize the benefits of such a seminar for maximizing the productivity of others on their team.

This strategy fails over the long term. Business success depends upon the ability to attract, train, and retain qualified people—and if you choose to ignore the management responsibilities in your job, you will experience high turnover of employees, which inevitably leads to a lack of productivity. Bad managers may be more intelligent than their peers but they will soon see their peers being promoted ahead of them.

Build Consensus and Trust

It is a general rule that people typically don't like being told what to do. Likewise, if you, as a manager, constantly tell your employees how to manage themselves, they will, eventually, stop thinking for themselves and then rely solely on your directions, which can be problematic for your time management and their productivity. People function best when they have a personal investment in a decision and understand the importance of what they are doing. Additionally, listen to the directions others give you as well, especially if they are more knowledgeable about the task and the best way to execute it. Building consensus will take a little more time up front but once a subordinate internalizes the need for a task, it will be performed to a much higher level of accuracy and efficiency.

I once read a transcript of a speech by Colin Powell in which he said that challenging possible decisions and giving input does not demonstrate a lack of loyalty but in fact, he highly encourages it. Once a decision is made, everyone must head in the same direction. If anyone challenges a decision after it has been made, then *that* shows a lack of loyalty. Therefore, you want to emphasize the important difference between giving your input before a decision has been made and effectively executing a decision once it has been made.

You also need to share information with those you are managing. The more data you can share that shows why you made a particular decision and how your department is functioning better due to that decision, the more your employees will trust you. This trust will reduce insubordination and encourage everyone to head in the same direction.

Look for Thoroughbreds

Thoroughbreds are the fastest, best horses. Mules, although functional in certain capacities, are the slowest. In the work world, you should look for employees who are thoroughbreds. Always try to hire as many thoroughbreds as you can. Your performance is based on the productivity of your department.

Another important process that affects the productivity of your department is to classify your employees as Bulls and Swans (as defined earlier in this chapter). Ensure that Bulls are properly challenged and focused on change initiatives. The Swans are very valuable for recurring tasks. If you switch these around, Bulls will get bored and Swans will become frustrated. Having a proper mix of these types of employees will vary based on the department, type of business, industry, and growth stage of the company. It is much easier to pull back on the reins of a thoroughbred than it is to whip a mule.

Reduce OPPs (Other People's Problems)

It is important to listen to your employees' problems and to be attentive to their needs, but OPPs can be the single biggest drain on your time as a manager. You need to focus on eliminating people who generate OPPs and reduce the number of individual occurrences of these types of employees. For example: If you manage a department of twenty people and each person has one problem per month that you are required to deal with (and each problem consumes one hour of your time), that means that one hour per workday will be consumed with OPPs . . . and that is a best-case scenario! Imagine if everyone had two or four problems each per month. You can see how having a frequent complainer on the job can quickly consume your time.

I once had a key employee who was extremely valuable. She knew everything about everything and I relied on her heavily because I was new to my position and the company. As time went on, I realized that everyone who reported to her was miserable, though. I also realized that she was constantly generating problems. I did not have enough experience to know what would happen if she were no longer in the department, but finally she decided to leave the company. I was very concerned how we would function going forward but was happily surprised when other staff members stepped up their performance and filled in around her responsibilities. We had one minor emergency shortly after she left but everyone pulled together and we handled it. Once I filled her position, the department's productivity and my own efficiency skyrocketed.

The moral of the story is to remove any person who consistently generates problems, regardless of how important they seem at the time, and your productivity and level of job satisfaction is sure to increase.

Watch Out for the Complainers

In situations of extreme stress, like plane crashes, people will react differently. Following are the different ways they will act:

- Some people will escape without regard for others.
- Others will help their neighbors get out.
- Most will do what others tell them to do.
- A few will panic and freeze.

The people who panic and freeze will cause the death of the people who try to help them.

Using this example, you must analyze your departmental employees. Most departments will have a few people with a positive attitude and a majority who will go with the flow. You will most likely have a few with a negative attitude. It is extremely important to identify these people early and to keep a close watch on them. If you do not get these negative thinkers headed in the right direction, they will begin to influence the bulk of the people in the middle. Do not take it as a personal failure if you cannot help these people to garner a positive attitude, because some people just tend to be negative and are difficult to help. Your job is to save as many employees as possible in your department from falling into this trap. Everyone needs to know that a negative attitude will not be tolerated, one way or the other.

Allow Subordinates to Make Mistakes

This is a delicate point because it is always important to do a job accurately. As a manager, you must allow for a work environment where people try to expand their capabilities and excel. When they extend their capabilities, however, some people will ultimately make mistakes. If you punish them harshly for these mistakes, their natural instinct is to withdraw into their comfort zone and not push themselves in the future. This means that you have now dramatically reduced the capacity and potential of that individual and the department as a whole.

This reminds me of when my accounting manager tried to do some important analyses that were going to be presented to the executive management and ownership. She spent many hours on it and was very proud of what she had done. When we went through it, though, we realized there were several errors in her report. Initially, she became very defensive, even though she knew she was wrong. When she noticed that I was not upset with her for making those errors, but instead was proud of her for trying because she got well over 90 percent of it correct, she was no longer defensive. She learned how to do the remaining part correctly before our meeting.

Additionally, I noticed her trying more complicated analyses in the future. Sure, she made some additional mistakes but it was the process of reviewing her work and correcting those mistakes that provided for the greatest learning opportunities. Had she been criticized for her mistakes, she would have never tried anything new and would not have excelled at her job.

You should evaluate your employees based on the number of mistakes that result from extending themselves. For every mistake, it probably means they had ten successes. If you see no mistakes, then they may not be pushing themselves hard enough to achieve true success.

Don't Talk Someone Out of Quitting

There are two reasons why people want to quit. First, they have found a better opportunity. Second, they are not happy. In the first scenario, it is your responsibility to make sure that your employees are challenged and compensated to the best of your abilities to reduce the number of people who seek better opportunities. Sometimes, people outgrow the opportunities you can offer; this should be seen as a compliment to you, and you need to then allow them the opportunity to grow elsewhere. By doing so, you will demonstrate that you respect their talents and that you are motivated to also help them achieve their goals; it's not only about what your employees can do for you. This attitude will raise the overall effectiveness and productivity of your department to the highest level possible.

If you notice an employee is performing at a lower level and that they exude general unhappiness, make yourself available to talk about the issue and try to help him resolve it so he does not feel trapped and then quit. If he has gotten to the point of quitting, he has done you the biggest favor in the world, actually. It is increasingly difficult to terminate an employee, so when an underperforming employee wants to leave, do *not* stop them.

What Were They Like on the Playgrounds?

Were your employees picked on as kids? Did they pick on others? Were they popular? Good team players? Or were they too smart for their own good? Getting a feel for what your employees were like as kids will help you better understand how they will react when working with others. If they were picked on, they are probably self-conscious and you will need to help boost their confidence. If they were a bully, you need to keep a close eye on them to make sure they are being supportive to everyone on the team.

Give Credit in Public, Criticize in Private

This is becoming a lost art in the modern business environment and is one of the biggest mistakes made by new managers today. Always remember to treat your subordinates the way you want to be treated. Do you like receiving praise in front of others? A lot of people will say no, but deep down, it does make them feel good. Do you like being criticized in front of others? Absolutely not.

Criticism must be delivered in private so that a person can be honest and introspective about the critique he or she is receiving. When done in public, the same person will become defensive and accusatory. Mistakes are merely learning opportunities if you handle them appropriately and in private.

Your Employees Must Feel Appreciated

You are responsible for creating an environment in which people want to be a part of your team. One of the most important elements of the work environment is for everyone to feel appreciated. As long as you openly appreciate everyone's efforts, your employees will work harder and be more productive for you. If they do not feel appreciated, these workers will eventually stop trying to please you. Apathy—and a decrease in productivity—is soon to follow.

Fire One, Fire Two, After That, It May Be You

I once had someone who worked for me who constantly accused her subordinates of not being able to do their jobs properly. Every time there was a problem, I was told it was someone else's fault. I allowed her to terminate the employee who was her biggest problem in the first few weeks I took over the department. Shortly thereafter, she wanted to terminate someone else. Upon informing me of this, I told her that I had no problem with that but to keep this in mind: Her job as a manager was to identify, hire, train, and retain employees. If she continued to fire subordinates, it would then start a trend that would reveal her incapability of identifying and training good employees. Therefore, the problem would be with her and not her subordinates. When she realized that she was not proficient at training and retaining her employees, she decided to take a different job, where she was not responsible for managing any employees.

Identify "C" Players and Move Them Up or Out

Many leaders make the mistake of keeping "C" players around because it is too difficult to get rid of them, or too painful. Vernon believes the bottom line is that leaders spend more time trying to improve the "C" players than moving the "B" players to "A" players. If you have a "C" player, make sure you have coached them appropriately for performance improvement. If, within a reasonable amount of time their performance does not improve, you must then make a decision to move them out. You may be doing them a favor in the long run. Leaving them on the team hurts the ability of the team to move forward and does not teach the weak employee how to develop better business skills.

Starting Your Own Business

The foundation of our economy that supports a large portion of innovation and job growth is small business. Many people dream of starting their own business. My million-dollar idea was Total Home Solutions. I felt there were plenty of people out there, particularly dual-income couples, who enjoyed living in a nice house but did not want to take care of it. My business partner and I developed a great business plan and decided to jump in with both feet. With my financial and sales background, I handled those particular responsibilities of our small business. His background was in IT and operations so those were his responsibilities. What a great fit. We were going to be millionaires . . . or so we dreamed.

A part of many people's lives is to have their careers progress from employee, to self-employed, to owning their own business. Following is advice from my own experience:

Don't Do It!

Let me first try and talk you out of it. If you make it to the next page, I will then help you make your idea become a reality. Following are several reasons why not to start your own business:

- The odds are against you. Only about 10 percent of new businesses succeed. And even if they do succeed, larger competitors have the ability to adapt and replicate your new product or service so fast that it is almost impossible to continue profitably in the long term.
- New businesses require a significant amount of your time—probably longer hours than you have ever worked in your life. If you have other time commitments in your life, this will quickly become a large source of time stress.
- Many new businesses are also based on working when most people want to be relaxing (i.e., nights and weekends). This is a bigger problem if you ever plan on being married and having children.
- If you have the skill set necessary to start your own business, you can probably make a much more secure living working for a company and utilizing those talents . . . and you will make more money!
- New businesses require money, and more than you initially estimate. Can you handle the financial loss you'll incur if the business fails? If not, you will need investors. The investors who pursue high-risk investments expect

high returns. This can put tremendous pressure on you as you begin your start-up.

- Legal, liability, and employee issues are very complex and difficult to properly handle in today's litigious environment.
- The administrative requirements are more burdensome than you may first realize.

Let me share the story of some friends of mine who wanted to have their own business. They were both engineers, making good money, and they had a son who was seven years old at the time. They decided to buy a party and gift store. They were working their normal jobs during the week, where they made much more money, and then on the weekends they were setting up bounce houses and delivering balloons all over the state. This was a tremendous drain on their time and they were actually losing money. After about two years and several operational adjustments, they finally decided to get their personal lives back (not to mention the money to cover their losses), so they shut the store down.

So I Was Not Able to Talk You Out of It

If the section above did not discourage you from starting your own business, it will be important to give you some advice for when you do set out to run things on your own. Before we start, know that many people never try to start a new business, or anything outside their comfort zone, because they are afraid to fail. The fact is, very few people succeed with their first try at starting their own business. Do not be discouraged by this process because you will learn several important lessons that will help you the next time you try. The following advice will help you dramatically improve your odds.

First, Better Than or Cheaper Than?

What is your idea for your start-up company? It needs to be one of the following:

- First—This is the best situation because you can get the highest profit margins (at least until competition enters your space). Some key questions to ask include:
  - Is anyone else doing this?
  - Why not?
  - How can you do it when someone else can't?
  - Will there be enough of a market to buy my product or service?
  - How fast could someone replicate this idea?
- Better than—With the way our economy is moving, this will generally apply to service businesses only. Many products are assembled abroad and important relationships need to be in place in order to build a better product for the consumer.
- Cheaper than—Once again, you should focus on services rather than products for the same reasons above. A good example of this type of business is when you have developed an expertise and decided to go out on your own (i.e., as an accountant, attorney, or IT consultant). You can cut out a lot of overhead and other people's profits when you offer your skills directly to customers. As your business grows and you need to hire others, it will be more difficult to remain cheaper than your competition.

Volume versus Margin

Are you going to make a little bit of money off a lot of customers or are you going to make a lot of money from a few clients? If you are relying on a few clients to pay a high margin, you will take on increased business risk. It will be more likely that competitors will enter your space and undercut your pricing.

Making a small margin from a high volume of customers will prevent competition and also protect you in the event some of your customers go elsewhere. You are not dependent on any individual customers this way and will have a great rate of success.

If It Doesn't Work on Paper, It Won't Work in Reality

Develop a business plan, financial model, and marketing plan. Have trusted and respected members of your network review these. They will help you think in ways you had not thought about yet. Test and challenge your assumptions. Create several different scenarios. All of these are important in helping you develop your idea during the "cheap" stage. If you can't get your idea to make money on paper, it certainly won't in reality . . . and you will spend a lot of money learning that lesson!

Make Sure the Timing Is Right

Some people have great ideas but the market is not ready to embrace them yet. This often happens with new technologies. Be sure you have enough money and a reasonable marketing plan in place before you jump out on your own. You can also do some test marketing to help validate your idea prior to spending a lot of capital to start your business.

You Need to Be a Ball Buster

There is a difference between being a good manager and leading a company. As a good manager you need to encourage everyone to function at their highest level and maintain a positive attitude. As a leader of an organization, the profitability and value of the company form the basis for how you are evaluated. Many leaders have the ability to drive people way beyond what is reasonable to expect.

If you decide to start a business where you will have employees, you better be able to drive people beyond their reasonable limits to ensure your profitability and success.

It Is the Administrative Tasks That Will Hurt You

Insurance, income tax, sales tax, payroll tax, contracts, workers' compensation, telephone systems, IT networks, and advertising collateral—in every job I had, these functions existed and seemed to run on autopilot. When starting your own business, however, you need to know about these basic administrative tasks or you have to pay someone to do them for you. Paying for others to do these dramatically cuts into your profitability. Make sure that you anticipate these expenses before you start. If you don't do it right at the beginning, it will cost you drastically more down the road.

Summary

Continuously improve the most important personal traits along with being the best manager possible so that you can maximize the effectiveness for 80,000 hours of your life.

Now that you understand how to create a solid foundation for your career, which will enable you to afford your desired lifestyle, it is time to address the next core element of life: relationships and marriage.

CHAPTER 8:
MARRIAGE AND ROMANTIC RELATIONSHIPS

One of the most fulfilling and rewarding parts of life is marrying the right person. Unfortunately, at the current time, a marriage only has a 50 percent chance of lasting (according to Jennifer Baker of the Forest Institute of Professional Psychology, the divorce rate in America is actually 50 percent for first marriages, 67 percent for second marriages, and 74 percent for third marriages). With all the information and technology that is available to us, you would think we would have a better marriage success rate.

The romantic and emotional side of marriage gets plenty of attention in society; we will discuss how the logistical side of marriage is actually the most critical to ensuring a lasting relationship and merits more attention from couples on a whole. One of the most important decisions you will make in your life is who you choose to be your spouse. In order to make a good decision, you must balance the emotional side of the relationship with an honest exploration of your logistical compatibility. By understanding and addressing your logistical compatibility, you will strengthen the emotional realm of your relationship. You must have both elements for a lasting and fulfilling marriage.

Admittedly, discussing logistical compatibility could not possibly sound less romantic! But if this is one of the most important decisions in life, shouldn't it be a good one? In my experience, there are three primary causes for dissatisfaction in a marriage that ultimately leads to divorce:

- **You made a bad choice**—Some people stay in a relationship too long. Both people know deep down in their hearts that the relationship will not last but they do not exit the relationship. Then, as more time is spent in the relationship, the couple receives social pressure to get married. This type of relationship is doomed and is one of the most disappointing wastes of time and effort because it was preventable.
- **The couple becomes incompatible over time**—Every relationship requires adjustments and compromises as each individual goes through changes over the years. As changes occur, partners need to work out strategies for adapting to these changes, or find a way to work on a course correction that is acceptable to both partners. This is a universal experience among long-term couples, so you must see the question as not whether you will grow apart but how you will manage it when you do in at least some respects. Say one spouse who loved the urban professional life may, over many years, decide that his or her undying dream is to move to the country to raise goats and become an artisanal cheese maker. You may have a strong loving relationship with your spouse; however, starting a goat farm with your partner may require you to give up the promotion you've worked five years to achieve. Love will not get you a

mutually acceptable result in this scenario; compromise will be required by one or both partners. These kinds of changes are not always anticipated, discussed, or agreed to prior to the wedding and thus can lead to a divorce later in life.

- **Financial problems**—Unrealistic financial expectations and the resulting stress have ruined many marriages. People who do not pay proper attention to their personal finances put their relationships at risk. This is because finances affect everything from where you live to what makes you happy to what you drive to what you do to what you wear and to what you eat. Without a sound financial foundation, there will not be much romance or partnership over the years.

Let's be perfectly honest: Marriage is hard work. Anyone who does not think so is making an incredibly bad decision when he or she decides to get married. In this chapter, I will share insights based on my personal experience and observations along with the many, many successful people I know that will help you to find a compatible spouse, maximize your relationship, and understand situations that may arise over the course of your relationship that many people are less likely to divulge to a newly married couple.

As we take you through the following advice and scenarios, do not mistake our honest discussion of working on logistical compatibility with your potential spouse for a negative view of marriage; we simply want to help you to maximize your chances of happiness and fulfillment in your relationships.

Finding a Compatible Spouse

A good friend of mine had one of the best sayings I ever heard relating to marriage. He said, "The only thing dumber than running out of gas is marrying the wrong person." It's true that marriage is perhaps the biggest decision you will ever make in your life. Choose the best spouse for you and life can be extremely fulfilling. Choose the wrong life partner and you may find yourself miserable, particularly if children are involved at a later stage. The following is extremely valuable advice to help you make better relationship decisions.

Marriage Is a Lot of Hard Work

Marriage requires much more work than I ever realized. I am very lucky to have married someone who puts in a lot of effort and is able to *compromise* to make our marriage a success. Many people grow up thinking that when they find the right person, marriage will be magical and they will live happily ever after. This is a dangerous assumption because the people who believe this fairy-tale ending are simply setting themselves up for a lifelong series of relationships full of disappointment. Later in this book you will learn about setting a reasonable level of expectations in order to be happy. When people set their expectations at a "fairy-tale" level, which is the highest level possible, they are virtually guaranteed to be disappointed.

A successful marriage demands a lot of effort, particularly during difficult times (and everyone will have them), and compromise. It also requires an openness to communicate your needs and to understand your spouse's needs. Marriage also requires the ability to apologize. The belief that love is enough to live happily ever after is simply not realistic; you need to be careful of becoming committed to a partner who believes the future will take care of itself simply because the "two of you are right for each other."

Be Friends

Early in a relationship, emotions are like an unbelievable fireworks show. Unfortunately, the show does not last forever at the same level as the first stage of infatuation. At some point, a husband and wife need to establish a good friendship and share common interests. The best way to describe the level a relationship must ascend to is a "partnership" because then it can survive the natural peaks and valleys that time will take it through. Your spouse needs to be your best friend or you will encounter difficulties down the road that could be detrimental to your relationship.

There Can Be No Romance without Finance

The first rule of a successful romance is to have adequate finances (I know, that's not very "romantic" sounding but it's true). Would you buy a car or a house or any other luxury item if you did not have the money to afford it? Of course not, so why would you get married without the adequate amount of money and earnings potential?

Are you an individual who values money as part of your marriage decision? Do you want a spouse who will, in all likelihood, make good money and will provide the lifestyle you envision? Then go to college and get a good job. College and a good job are needed for several reasons:

- People attract and are attracted to other people with similar qualifications and values.
- Very few financially successful couples meet in high school.
- Half of financially successful couples meet in college and the other half meet after college because their future paths were more closely aligned.
- Dual-income marriages are more common and will continue to increase in popularity.
- A good education and career will provide for a healthy balance of power in your relationship.
- Wealthy men usually marry women with good jobs and/ or good educations.
- If you become divorced or widowed someday, you will need to provide for yourself.

Three Warnings Signs before Getting Serious

These are the three warning signs to be aware of when you are dating. One of these alone does not kill a relationship, but if your relationship has two or all three, pull the rip cord and get out of there:

- **Living at home**—This is a warning sign of unrealistic expectations. This person is looking to move into a place that is the same or better than where they currently live. They are also not used to taking care of their home and paying bills. Unless you can provide this environment (and at this stage you probably can't), be careful. This will surely cause financial stress for you.
- **Inability to compromise**—Marriage is a lot of hard work and requires a willingness to make sacrifices. Watch out

for someone who has the characteristics of a stereotypical "only child" who is used to having the world rotate around him or her. You will have to make many more sacrifices in this relationship than if you marry someone who has the ability to compromise.

- **Sexual compatibility**—It is paramount to talk at length about sexuality and maybe even experiment prior to making a commitment. Be sure that there is sexual compatibility before you get married, and be selective in who you choose to test the waters with beforehand. Promiscuity and not using the proper proactive measures can be damaging.

Don't Get Married before Twenty-three

What is the rush? When people get married too early, each spouse can still be overly influenced and supported by their parents. Before you settle down, it is important to know how your potential spouse functions on their own, away from their parents and from the comforts of college life. Life will change dramatically between high school and the real world. It is rare that a relationship will be able to adapt to these changes without one person holding the other back. Also, relationships are like many other parts of our lives where we need to learn from trial and error. Do not hold on to a relationship too tightly if there is not a future for it. Don't worry; there are plenty of people out there.

In their teens and early twenties, men and women need to focus on building a strong foundation for life by acquiring the best education possible and getting a good start on their career. Only then can marriage be considered. In a survey of financially successful couples I initiated for this book, I found that only 4 percent of married respondents met in high school; half met in college; and the other half met after college. The average age of our financially successful couples was twenty-five when they got married (this average age would likely be even higher if you are in a major metropolitan area). Don't let a relationship inhibit you from making the necessary transition from high school to college and then on to the working world.

You Are Also Marrying Your In-laws

A successful relationship requires each spouse to accept and be accepted by their in-laws. In a perfect world, this really should not matter. In the real world, however, in-laws can be a major influence in deciding the success of a relationship. Additionally, there will be family gatherings in which everyone will need to put up with each other in a civil manner. If children are involved, having a civil relationship with your in-laws can make it easier to ask for help with babysitting or other child-related factors.

Don't Get Married Just to Have Children

It is important that both people in the relationship either want to have children or not. If either partner has reservations about having children, this is a conflict that needs to be resolved prior to marriage. That being said, do not get married *just* to have children. Children can be the single greatest cause of stress on a marriage and can cause division rather than togetherness. The relationship must be strong prior to having children. You can buy many books and attend many seminars about marriage and parenting. You can have daydreams about having children. Just about every parent and expert would agree that the extraordinary challenges of raising and caring for children will easily crush a relationship that lacks a thorough, time-tested commitment. Be warned that children won't bring you together, especially if your relationship is already rocky; if you lack a strong foundation prior to adding an additional person in the mix, the added stress and time demanded by children will tear you apart.

From infancy to adolescence, your children become your priority, and your independent time will never be the same. You need a strong, trusted partner for this job; if you want to raise children with a spouse, start with a deep reservoir of mutual respect, love, and shared life experience.

Living Together before Marriage Has Become More Common

Before the 1970s (roughly speaking), unmarried couples living together was frowned upon. In our modern society, however, this practice has become more common and more widely accepted. The main benefit of living together is to "test-drive" your relationship. You will learn whether you are compatible with the other person before you make the major commitment of marriage. People who decide to live together before marriage will find it very difficult to exit this relationship if problems arise, though, so evaluate the strengths and weaknesses of your relationship before you begin living together, or the result will be several prime years of wasted time before the relationship finally ends.

Watch Out for Early Bloomers

Though we sometimes think early bloomers are the most successful, this is not always the case. People who are early bloomers, in many cases, do not develop as much of a personality or drive to succeed because they have never had to rely on those traits in the past. The best person to meet is a late bloomer. They are every bit as attractive as an early bloomer except they have developed a personality. In addition, early bloomers tend to expect opportunities to come to them rather than seeking them out. This worked early for them but will lead to great frustration later in life.

Write Down What You Like (Not Just Love)

Potential partners need to resolve core issues including children, religion, personal interests, and where to live prior to getting married. Many people enter into a prenuptial agreement prior to marriage so they are prepared for an easier divorce if one should arise in the future. Instead of anticipating a separation, however, I want to help you plan for success in your marriage. Figure out what you *like* about each other and the strengths that you want to stay the same. Then figure out what needs to change between the two of you.

If couples can learn some lessons from how successful companies merge, it will help their relationship succeed. When companies merge, they look at their processes, strengths, and weaknesses. They select the areas of each company that have the best processes and strengths. They then merge the weaker areas into the stronger company. This is a similar approach to what a couple should do. What are each partner's strengths? What are their weaknesses? What do they like about each other? What makes them happy? What needs to change? Who is going to have the dominant role in the various areas? If you work through this process before you get married, and both partners come to a point of mutual agreement, then you will dramatically increase your odds of a successful, lifelong partnership.

To help bridge this gap, we have developed a template to help you identify the qualities you like in your relationship that you want to continue into marriage, and to recognize those areas that you and your partner should work on changing. This will make it easier for future spouses to stay together rather than providing for an easier exit like a prenuptial agreement. I have included this Marriage Compatibility worksheet on the next page to help with this process (a user-friendly version is also available at TheSuccessGift.com). When this worksheet is completed and everything has been agreed to, make ten copies and hide them everywhere for future reference.

Marriage Compatibility Worksheet

	Husband	Wife
Major Decisions: Do you want children? - If so, how many, when, and how involved will you be? What religion will you raise children? Where will you live? How involved will each family (in-laws) be?		
Financial Decisions: How big of a house do you want to live in (now, 10 years, 20 years)? Will you work when we get married? Will you work when we have children? After they are grown? Would you relocate for a job opportunity for your spouse? Is it more important to have a nice house or children at a young age? Do you realize how expensive children are? What major material possessions will you want? When? What can you live without having?		
Time Decisions: What hobbies, activities, or interests does your spouse have that they will need to reduce time previously spent doing? Is the amount of time your spouse spends at work reasonable? If we have children and you decide not to work: - will you understand the need for working late? - will you do what you can to take care of the stresses of the house? - will you do what you can to take care of the stresses of children?		
What makes you happy? What makes you happy? What are your favorite things about your spouse? What do you want to change when you get married? How often do you have sex now? In 5 years? 10 years? How neat are you? What household responsibilities will you have? What responsibilities do you expect your spouse to have? What do you already consider a sacrifice? Is there anything else that is important to you that is not covered above?		
What goals do you have? How successful do you want to be in your career? What important achievements do you want to accomplish? When? Is there anything else that is important to you that is not covered above?		

Maximize Your Relationship

Once you have found your spouse and have decided to get married, you must work to ensure that you have a successful marriage. Always remember that no one is perfect and everyone will go through many changes and difficult situations that cannot be anticipated at any time. Working hard at your relationship will always be required, as will flexibility.

You Now Have 336 Hours!

A special advantage of being married is that you now have 336 hours per week in which to complete tasks and increase your productivity. To maximize the success of your marriage, allocate this time to accentuate the strengths of each partner. I was watching *The Today Show* while writing this book and saw a special on stay-at-home spouses. The interviewer asked a young wife who is childless at the moment how she is enjoying staying at home. She said, "I am very happy but my husband is not doing his half of the chores around the house." My head almost exploded when I heard this!

We recommend that you use business terms to help you and your spouse understand your roles in marriage. A great deal of marriage deals with financial and administrative affairs. It's practically a small business in itself. Consider the business functions that exist in a relationship: revenue generating, maintenance, customer service, and accounting. The person who generates the most revenue ("Provider") needs to spend as much time as possible doing that. The other person ("Caretaker") needs to handle as many functions and responsibilities as they can to free up the time of the revenue generator.

Also, know the value of the revenue generator's time. If she does not have an hourly wage, you can calculate this by taking her annual salary and dividing it by 2,000 hours (the number of hours in a typical work year). When something needs to be done, and it will cost less than what the revenue generator could make in that time period, strongly consider outsourcing that project to save both of you the extra time and energy.

Knowing When You Got to the Right Decision

This classic quote came from a well-respected former coworker who once said, "I always know when my wife and I have reached the right decision. It is when neither of us is happy." Though this sounds somewhat sad, this statement is actually rather accurate. Marriage is about compromise and negotiation. If one spouse always expects to be happy, that person will become sorely disappointed and this may lead to future marital problems or even divorce.

You Can Outsource Everything Except Sex

As stated above, it is important that you marry someone who is sexually compatible with you. If your partner is not, then you need to make a choice: either leave or learn how to make yourself more compatible to your partner. All too often people look outside of their relationships to supplement their sexual desires—whether strictly for sex or for some other reason, such as loneliness, power, or excitement. This is the one area that cannot be outsourced without causing significant and permanent damage to your long-term relationship. People who have successful relationships continue to work on ways to keep the romance alive and also respect each other enough to talk through any sexual problems they may be having.

Women Want to Change Men, but Men Want to Stay the Same

I never realized I did so many things wrong in life until I got married. The first year of my marriage, in particular, required dramatic changes from me as my wife and I went through the process of developing a compatible lifestyle. I cleaned more, bought real furniture (milk crates were no longer a "cool" look), decorated our home, and learned things like what a "valance" is. I am not sure how it happens but women seem to be much more prepared for marriage than men.

Situations That No One Talks About

Your parents told you how great having children was for them. Unfortunately, they failed to tell you the truth because they did not have the heart to divulge what a pain you actually were to raise. And, in most cases, the world of working and the world of raising kids are both more demanding today than they were when your parents were raising you. Children can make a marriage more fulfilling but they are not a cure for marital difficulties and challenges. The reason for this is surprisingly simple. It takes a lot of time to raise children properly. In addition, there are a lot of expenses incurred in order to properly feed, clothe, and care for your child. Since time and money are finite resources, you will need to reallocate the ways you previously spent your time and money. This can be a very challenging process. This is why your marriage and financial situation need to be rock solid before you decide to have children.

Each Spouse Is Chronically Underappreciated

The world has become so complicated and everyone seems to be running at 100 miles per hour. When this happens, people tend to get tunnel vision and focus only on what they need and want to get done. The needs of others, particularly a spouse, tend to become minimized. When this inevitable cycle occurs in a busy household, the other person feels underappreciated. The irony is that this person is usually treating his spouse the same way, albeit perhaps in a different context, and he probably doesn't realize it. Part of the hard work and compromise that goes into a relationship is making a specific effort to recognize the good things your spouse does on a daily basis. Also make an effort to spend uninterrupted time together so that any negative feelings can be discussed at an early stage, which will enable a couple to reconnect and reassess their priorities.

Decision to Stay at Home—the Modern Framework

Many of us grew up in a home where the father was the Provider and the mother was the Caretaker. Once the children got a little older, the wife may have taken a part-time job, such as working at a school, so that she could receive extra income and still be available when her children were on school vacation. Today, however, things have become much more complicated.

Presently, most families rely on two incomes in order to afford the needs, conveniences, and luxuries that many couples want. Additionally, now that the business environment has been leveled, it will become more and more common that the wife will have more earnings potential than her husband. There are also more options to care for children without fully sacrificing either parent's career, such as hiring a nanny or all-day childcare. The decision to stay home now mainly relies on this question: Do you need more money or less time stress?

I did not understand this need fully until it happened to me. My wife has a very successful career and she was presented with a great opportunity to relocate. Since my schedule was flexible at the time, we decided to move. At the time this opportunity arose, we had a nanny for our children. Our nanny was fantastic and the children loved her. However, since we were relocating, we decided to let the nanny go prior to our move, so the children would have time to adjust to the new arrangement.

This decision turned out to be the most difficult for me because I never considered that I would stay at home with my children; but I finally realized that staying home was the right decision as we had the income to cover our lifestyle costs and it was more important to me and my wife that I stay with the children.

Stay-at-home Dads Will Be More Common

Women in a corporate officer role for Fortune 500 companies were practically nonexistent a few decades ago. Through progressive laws and attitude changes, women comprised around 11 percent of the corporate officer roles in 1998 and increased to 16 percent in 2008 (according to Catalyst, the not-for-profit New York–based women's research organization). There are many challenges for these working women, but one of the most significant is balancing work and family. How can a woman dedicate the same amount of time at work as her male counterparts and still be considered a successful wife and mother? Many couples are coming to the realization that the wife has more earnings potential than the husband, and this forces them to address the issue of how to handle the Caretaker responsibilities.

As these couples go through the process of solving this issue, a common solution becomes apparent—the husband will become the Caretaker.

I became one of these Caretaker husbands. When my wife relocated for work, I was faced with the job of becoming the Caretaker. When I was growing up, I never once thought that I would be in this role and have the primary responsibility of raising my children. Once my wife and I thought through everything, though, we made the decision that I would become a stay-at-home dad. Once I stepped in to this role, I started to realize how many other fathers were taking on the same responsibilities in their respective households.

I believe that as more fathers assume the Caretaker role, and it becomes more socially acceptable, we will see more women in top executive roles. It is extremely difficult to make it to the top without the proper support system. As a relationship is formed, this is a scenario that needs to be considered by both parties. If the wife has the potential to make more money, is the husband willing to take a more active role in raising the future children?

Summary

Now that you have a solid understanding of the logistical side of marriage, it is important to add the emotional and romantic side back in. You need *both* the emotional connection and the logistical compatibility for your marriage to be a success—if you posses both of these, you will maximize this fulfillment in your life. The next core element of life, your home, follows.

CHAPTER 9:
HOME

The traditional definition of the American Dream has always included a home with a white picket fence that houses a husband, wife, and 2.2 children. Of course, everyone has their personal definition of this dream, based on their desired lifestyle, the economic situation, and other things unique to their lives. However, our point is that "owning your own home" has, for many reasons, become the foundation of how people think about economic security and general well-being. We now know that despite the many benefits of home ownership, over the past decade home mortgage "ownership" was oversold and overhyped, ultimately becoming a significant cause of the economic crash in 2008. The government had encouraged its citizens to buy houses in the years past. Thus, people believed they needed to own a home in order to provide their families with an adequate, American lifestyle (some even thought they needed to own more than one home). Investors bought several homes because prices were quickly rising. Then reality hit and the market realized that everyone who could afford a home already owned one! It also turned out—not so surprisingly to many of us—that the market realized a significant number of people owned homes who had no chance of being able to afford them. This caused a flood of available homes on the market and a classic case of economics took over. When supply increases dramatically, prices drop. And they dropped hard!

In this chapter you will learn:

- The benefits of buying versus renting a home.
- How to select a home.
- Ways of getting the most out of your home.

Buying versus Renting a Home

The key to whether you should own your home or simply rent one comes down to two simple questions:

- Will I be here for at least five years?
- Can I afford the home and continue my desired lifestyle?

If the answer is "no" to either of those questions, rent! Yes, that's right, I said rent. Renting can be an excellent decision and it is utterly underappreciated. When something breaks, you simply call the landlord and it is taken care of for you. If you don't like your location, you can easily move at the end of the lease to a different complex or part of town. Think about all the perks of apartment living: no yard work (and, therefore, no need to buy pricey lawn equipment), appliances that are already provided for, and a pool, tennis court, and workout facility (in some cases). It is easy living!

If you do not want to rent, or feel that you would like yard work, new appliances, and your own backyard pool, you may start down the path of homeownership. If you are going to be successful in purchasing a home, however, you need to demonstrate to yourself and others that you have reasonable career and financial stability. Why is this so important? First, buying, furnishing, and maintaining a home is expensive. The money required to meet the basics of homeownership is always more than the first-time homeowner expects. Second, if you want to sell your home in the future, you will once again be surprised by the expenses and intense stress this process creates. People who will be living in a home for less than five years will likely lose money on their significant investment when the time comes for them to relocate. If you are going to lose money and have more headaches, why would you want to own a home at the present time?

In the following section, we provide essential guidelines for those of you who have the money to purchase, the time to properly care for, and the stability needed in your life to own a home. As you read through this chapter, keep in mind that if there are *any* areas that cause an issue for you, you should be renting and not buying. Renting is a fantastic way to limit stress and free up your finances for other goals and incentives.

Selecting a House

The first step in shopping for a house is finding enough money for a down payment and some extra cash for a financial cushion. A general rule of thumb is that you should pay 20 percent of the purchase price in cash and have several thousand dollars more for the initial costs related to buying a home (i.e., repairs, improvements, and furnishing). Once that is accomplished, you are ready to start the process of buying a home. The following are some helpful tips with this process:

Do Not Choose Your Realtor Casually

As you would in selecting a doctor, attorney, accountant, or therapist, research the person you will choose to guide you through this transaction. First, you should recognize the difference between a real estate agent and a Realtor. A Realtor has specific qualifications and ethical standards they have met that are much higher than that of a real estate agent. A Realtor is also part of a Realtor Association that provides a grievance process for the home buyer or seller to go through if they are not satisfied with the performance of a particular Realtor. That being said, there are many Realtors out there and many people assume they are all the same. They are not! Selecting the right Realtor is essential. Check references, designations (i.e., GRI, CRS, ABR), look at their previous selling and buying experience, make sure they are familiar with your area of interest, ensure they have a solid reputation, and interview several of them before choosing one.

A Realtor will help guide you through the home-buying process. This does not dismiss any one of their clients from taking personal responsibility, however. Clients need to take personal responsibility to understand the process and to ensure that the Realtor is doing what is in the client's best interest. When buying a home, you are making one of the largest, if not *the* largest, financial commitment of your life. It never hurts to double (or even triple) check the information you are given to make sure it is accurate and appropriate for you.

On the buying side, there is no reason to sign an agreement to exclusively commit to a Realtor. The Realtor needs to maintain your trust in them, and if this trust is lost, having the flexibility to change will be extremely important for you.

Stay within a Budget

No home you can "own" with the help of a bank is worth high levels of financial stress. High levels of financial stress will damage your health, marriage, and long-term career. The joy of living in a home does not outweigh financial stress. There are many people who file for divorce due to overwhelming financial stress. First and foremost, it is very rare that any home will fit your needs perfectly, so understand that as you begin your search. And if a home does fit mostly all of your needs, the cost is likely way outside of your desired price range. You must establish reasonable expectations before stating the process of buying a home.

When my wife and I were looking for a home in Southlake, Texas, we gave the real estate agent a specific price range we needed to stay within. She showed us a few homes in that range and then showed us some above our range. We obviously liked the more expensive homes better, and once we saw these homes, it was more difficult to look at the ones in our original range. As a result, we bought a home that was above our range. It put us in a tight financial position for several years. Fortunately, this was in the late 1990s when salaries were going up rather quickly. We were lucky that we finally worked our way out of that financial hole but many people are not that fortunate, and I don't condone our behavior.

It's true: My wife and I fell into a common trap. Remember that any real estate agent (or home builder) and mortgage banker is a commissioned salesperson. They will try to sell you the biggest (and most expensive) home possible. People generally qualify for a loan that is far higher than what they should commit to in light of the other expenses in their lives. When buying a home, you must prepare a budget (as discussed in chapter 4). This will show you exactly how much can be spent on buying a home—and then you must stick to it.

An indication of whether or not someone should be buying a home is the interest rate on the proposed mortgage. If the interest is a higher rate than what most people are receiving, the bank is trying to tell you that you should not be buying a home at this particular time. This higher rate reflects the fact that your credit score needs to be improved and you do not possess enough financial stability to successfully mortgage a purchase of this caliber. When your credit score and financial stability improve, the interest rate will go down. It's key to know that a home purchased at a higher rate will likely drive the homeowner (you) into financial trouble in the future.

In addition to the monthly mortgage payment, the homeowner is also responsible for the cost of repairs inside and outside of the home. Most new homeowners underestimate how much it costs to maintain a home. This is the reason why renting is an advantage for many. When you rent and there is a problem, someone else pays for it!

Don't blame the banks for the higher interest rate because they are actually trying to do you a favor. You, in turn, need to be savvy and recognize the amount of money you are able to realistically put into a home and whether or not this is a viable option for you at the present time.

Think Resale When Buying a House

When buying a home, you need to consider not only how it fits your lifestyle but whether it will be easy to sell if that need arises. Many people do not think this far in advance and bite when they see a "great deal." Following are some tips:

- Location, location, location—These are the three most important factors people consider. Homes with short commuting distances, cul-de-sac lots, and large backyards are usually most attractive. Avoid areas with a lot of traffic that neighbor commercial properties, are close to bad neighborhoods, are located in such a way that headlights shine directly into the house at night, or are near overhead power lines. Also consider the quality of the public schools in the area. Even if you do not have children, people who will eventually buy your home will likely have them.
- Buy a smaller home in a higher-priced neighborhood rather than the most expensive home in a neighborhood.
- The parts of the house that impact resale most are the kitchen, master bedroom, and landscaping.
- Paint and carpet are easy to change but everything else can be challenging. When buying a "fixer-upper," make sure that it only needs cosmetic repairs and not anything structural (an independent inspection is essential).

Select a Licensed Inspector

As with other sectors of the real estate industry during the 1997–2008 economic boom, the home inspection profession lost some of its integrity. Many home inspectors compromised and looked the other way during real estate transactions. No one wanted to switch the yellow signal on the real estate money train. Inspectors who raised too many issues and slowed down too many deals often lost business. As with the rating agencies on Wall Street, many home inspectors caved into the pressures of the deal and rubber-stamped the inspection. Obviously, many home inspectors did their job the right way, and many more inspectors have learned the error of their ways and returned to good, solid practices.

However, this is another reason why selecting a quality Realtor is so important; the *licensed* inspector is often recommended by the real estate agent. Always use a licensed inspector under any and all circumstances. Talk to several licensed inspectors before selecting the right one for you. Ensure that the licensed inspector will raise all important issues that would be helpful to know prior to purchasing a home. The licensed inspector will obviously address areas that are broken or outside of code. They should also address areas that will be difficult and expensive to maintain in the future.

Even new homes need an independent inspection. There are many corners that a builder can cut. Use the expertise these inspectors bring to the table in order to know exactly what is being purchased and how costly maintenance will be in the future.

Warranties Are Not as Good as They Seem to Be

The six- or twelve-month warranty that often comes with a home when it is purchased is primarily in place to protect the real estate agent and the previous homeowner (if you are buying an older house). If the house turns out to be a lemon, the real estate agent and home seller do not want to be sued in the aftermath.

Many people do not properly maintain their home because they believe that everything is covered by the warranty. After purchasing a home, it is the responsibility of the homeowner to properly maintain the home. Most problems that arise after purchasing a house are due to improper or inadequate home maintenance and those are generally not covered by a warranty.

Read the fine print carefully!

How Long Is the Commute?

Suburban America is sprawling farther outside of cities due to new housing developments built to accommodate population growth. There is a definite allure to a new home; additionally, the price per square foot is usually lower the farther the home is from the city because the land costs less. One problem is that the commute into the city for work or for other essentials (such as a grocery store, pharmacy, etc.) may be much longer than anticipated. If this commute is too long, it will increase your time stress and reduce your level of happiness and should be taken into strong consideration when you set out to purchase a home.

A great way to understand the commute that will be involved when living in the suburbs is to get up early on a workday and drive to the area you are looking to purchase a home in. Then drive the route to your office. This will help you calculate how long it will take you to get to work, not just how far you are from the office. Then do this after work one day as well. You will discover time-stressing issues, such as highways merging from three to two lanes and the volume of rush-hour traffic heading in your desired direction. Rush-hour traffic can add a significant amount of time onto your commute and it's better to be aware of this before you purchase a home and assess whether or not you can handle the daily commute without stress and dissatisfaction.

Do You Have the Time?

Homes can cause time stress in a variety of ways, primarily because they must be properly maintained. When repairs go unaddressed, they only get worse (read: bigger and more expensive). "Fixer-uppers" can completely drain a homeowner of all his or her free time (and money), especially if the homeowner lacks the skills to do the work properly the first time. Now throw some young children in the mix and the homeowner will go nuts trying to stay ahead of everything that needs to be done. Maintaining a home can be difficult and is often underestimated.

If you dislike doing house or yard work, factor into your financial equation the cost of hiring a cleaning and landscaping service to handle these needs for you. If you cannot afford to pay others to maintain your home—and you know you will not have the time or energy to do it yourself—you should rethink your home buying until you can afford to pay for these services.

Do You Have the Ability to Maintain Your Home?

Please be honest with yourself about the home maintenance issues. Ask yourself (and your partner or spouse if you are buying the house with them), "Do I have the ability? Do I have the desire?" or "Do I have a good friend who can teach me?" If not, buy a smaller home and outsource the maintenance. If you and your partner or spouse are willing to tackle maintenance, we recommend becoming great friends with any neighbor who has a variety of tools. Having the right tools and knowing how to use them is the key to success.

Big Houses Are Expensive Because You Have to Fill Them!

Everyone wants a big new home. Big homes cost a lot of money, though, and in addition to this, homeowners also have to fill all the space inside. I used to own a company that took care of upscale homes. Whenever I met with potential clients, I always met them at their respective houses. As soon as I walked in, I could tell immediately whether or not I wanted to work with them. If their home was not adequately furnished, it was obvious that they were in over their heads and were going to look to cut corners. There are no corners to cut when properly maintaining a home. You can pay now or pay more later.

Buy a home that is affordable for you to furnish and properly maintain. Why would anyone want to live in an empty, run-down house?

Getting the Most Out of Your Home

Congratulations on buying your home. Now, here are a few helpful tips I would like to share that will boost your enjoyment of your home and neighborhood. First and foremost, there are many good books on properly maintaining a home . . . buy one! The following tips are not covered in most books and should be taken to heart.

Make Friends with the Neighbor Who Has the Tools

The key to all home-repair projects is having the right tools. And it seems as though every street includes at least one neighbor who has an excellent set of tools. Many homeowners struggle with the problem that many tools are too specific to a type of project that is only performed one time. When that happens, it is not cost effective to buy the necessary tool(s). It can also be tricky to figure out how to properly use the tool if you've had no previous experience operating it. If your neighbor has that particular tool, he probably knows how to use it, too.

Compensation is usually paid in the form of future favors—or beer—so get out there and meet the new neighbors (and check out their garages as well)!

Proactive Maintenance Will Reduce Your Costs and Hassles

Almost everything we do in our lives has a proactive maintenance plan, like caring for a car, going to the dentist, or getting a physical from a doctor. Our home will be the largest single investment for most of us. With homes, people tend to have a "break and fix" mentality. Could you imagine having this attitude with your car? Just as you would with your car, look for early warning signals of potential home damage and then be proactive in making the necessary small fixes to avoid more costly and inconvenient repairs down the road. I have attached a sample Proactive Maintenance Plan on the next page that you should customize to your home (a user-friendly version is also available at TheSuccessGift.com).

Proactive Home Maintenance Plan (sample)

	Jan	Feb	Mar	Apr	May	Jun	Jul	Aug	Sep	Oct	Nov	Dec
Interior:												
Clean home	X	X	X	X	X	X	X	X	X	X	X	X
Carpet cleaning		X						X				
Window washing			X						X			
Home computer		X		X		X		X		X		X
Drapery cleaning					X							
Fire extinguisher	X			X			X			X		
Fireplace/flues									X			
Pest control		X			X			X			X	
Kitchen vents		X		X		X		X		X		X
First aid kit	X						X					
Furniture											X	
Mattress turn				X						X		
Natural stone				X								
Tile/tub/shower	X											
Change time on clocks			X							X		
Piano tuning		X						X				
Reverse Ceiling Fans			X							X		
Replace backup batteries			X									
Electrical						X						
Equipment & plumbing:												
Air filter change	X			X			X			X		
Air conditioning seasonal maint			X									
Air conditioning Maintenance						X		X				
Heating system seasonal Maint									X			
Hot water heater test & drain						X						X
Sprinkler system			X			X			X		X	
Garage door		X										
Plumbing - Check leaks		X			X			X			X	
Plumbing - Flush Lines					X						X	
Security system	X											
Smoke alarm system	X											
Septic tank										X		
Water Purification/Supply					X						X	
Other appliances		X						X				
Pond filters		X			X			X			X	
Small Engines			X									
Water Main connections												
Exterior:												
Mow & edge			X	X	X	X	X	X	X	X		
Pool cleaning	X	X	X	X	X	X	X	X	X	X	X	X
Fertilize			X		X		X		X		X	
Trim hedges				X		X		X		X		
Rake leaves											X	X
Seasonal flowers			X			X				X		
Tree Trimming	X											
Tree Feeding				X								
Doors/Windows				X						X		
Driveway							X					
Fence					X							
Foundation											X	
Gutter												X
Masonry	X						X		X			
Siding	X						X					
Outdoor pipes			X								X	
Roof				X						X		
Wood					X							

Recurring versus Nonrecurring Projects

If a project is recurring (like mowing the yard), invest in the proper tools. Additionally, take the time to become an expert—and begin by testing out an area of your house or yard that will not be seen, in case you botch up the project. For example, my wife wanted to faux paint our living room. We knew we did not have the skills and confidence to do this, so we faux painted our guest room first. We started in a corner that could not be seen when first entering the room. Then we worked our way toward the area that was most visible. Upon successful completion, we then faux painted our living room and did an outstanding job.

If a project is nonrecurring and too much of a hassle to do yourself, pay someone else to do it. By the time the tools are bought and experience is built, someone else could have been done already. This will also save you the cost of paying someone to fix the problems you created by trying to do a task yourself without the proper skill set.

Water Damage Is Almost Worse than Fire Damage

If you have a major water leak in your house, you may wish that your house had actually burned down instead. The hassle of repairing water damage is excruciating. Additionally, mold is a major concern in some parts of the country where water damages a home. Any significant water damage may impact the ability to sell or insure a home in the future. Whenever a repair involves plumbing, seriously consider employing an expert to fix the problem.

Respect Your Neighbor's Investment

This seems like common sense but too many people don't do it. When buying a home, embrace the responsibility of maintaining and beautifying your home so that the neighborhood maintains its value. You are buying a home *and* making an investment. That investment *can* be influenced by your neighbors—both positively and negatively. Homeowners need to make sure their home and lot receives adequate time, attention, and resources to protect this investment. If you do not take care of your house and property, you—without realizing, perhaps—negatively affect your neighbor's investment, and vice versa.

Don't Be Penny Wise, Pound Foolish

A homeowner can either pay now or pay even more later when it comes to repairs and maintenance. You will save money in the long run if you fix things immediately and do it right the first time. You need to be sure to have some money put aside to cover unexpected household expenses that you will undoubtedly encounter down the road. Homes that lack adequate resources to fix problems as they occur will start a negative financial cycle for their owners because the repairs can get dramatically more expensive as the problem gets bigger. Always be prepared to cover any problem that arises immediately.

Strategy for Furnishing Your Home

When furnishing a home, you should have a master plan of what you would like to do, then get the essentials first (bed, dresser, couch, television, and kitchen table). Look to the future when doing this so that these pieces will not need to be replaced later due to poor quality or inefficiency. Once the essentials have been obtained, go room by room, from most used to least used, and begin to furnish each. Be sure that pieces are purchased at the same level as everything else.

A cost-effective way of getting a significant portion of the initial furnishings for your home is to attend estate and garage sales. The depreciation for furniture is much worse than cars—and this you can use to your advantage. Used furniture costs *much* less than if you buy it new and can be rather unique as well.

When decorating a home, one of the cheapest ways to make an impact is by painting. Painting takes time but the cost is limited to a few gallons of paint and some brushes, rollers, and drop cloths. Remember to stay relatively neutral when choosing paint. A home is also an investment and bold statements are rarely valued by potential future buyers.

A quick tip I learned on making a room look well-decorated without spending a lot is that only the main pieces require a significant investment. After that, you can fill in with less expensive decorations.

Will I Like My Neighbors?

I would like to end this chapter with a story: Once there was a young couple looking for a new home. They saw a cute home in a nice neighborhood. There was an old couple working in the yard next door, so the young couple went over to talk to the pair. They inquired of the old couple as to if they would like this new neighborhood.

The old couple asked them how they liked their former neighborhood. The young couple said they were excited to be moving because they didn't have many friends in their old neighborhood, since the people were unfriendly and acted snobbish. The old couple said, "Unfortunately, this neighborhood is very much the same as your old one."

Disappointed, the young couple drove off with their realtor to look at some other houses.

Then another couple came by to look at the same house and saw the same the old couple. The new couple asked the same question to the older couple and they replied, "How did you like your old neighborhood?" To this the young wife started to tear up and said, "We are so sad to be leaving because our neighbors are such good friends and great people but my husband received a job opportunity that he simply couldn't turn down."

The older couple looked at them and said, "Don't worry because, fortunately, this neighborhood is very much the same as your old one."

The moral of this story is that only *you* can determine how much you will enjoy your neighborhood.

Summary

Now that you understand the intricacies of owning versus renting a home, it is time to address the final core element of life—children.

CHAPTER 10:
CHILDREN

The Waltons, Bradys, Ingalls, Huxtables, and Seavers—can you name the classic television series where each of these families is the focal point? These famous TV families stand as examples of "perfect" families and because of their influence, many people tend to view their families as having to fit the molds and constructs of these great (albeit fake) households. A crucial part of the "perfect" family revolved around children, who are viewed as helping to create a fulfilling life. And it is true that children can be the single greatest source of joy and happiness in our lives.

If you have children at the wrong time, though, your life will be significantly more challenging for you, your child, and those around you. This is because children create a strain on both your time and money. Having a child before you are in the right financial situation and mental state is one of the single biggest mistakes a couple can make.

At the beginning of this chapter I am going to make sure you have all the information necessary to assess whether or not you are in the proper life situation before you decide to have children. Upon making sure that you are ready, I will then share some observations that will help you when you do finally have children.

Deciding to Have Children

Everyone has the *right* to have children but too many people fail to understand that once they exercise that *right*, they also have the *responsibility* to properly raise those children. If you are not able to fulfill that responsibility, then you should not have a child. Work hard to put yourself in the situation where you can handle the responsibility, and then you can bring children into the mix. Both you and your child will have a much easier and fulfilling life if you do things in order and at the proper time.

It is important that you understand whether you are in a position to handle the responsibility of raising children. If you do not plan appropriately, it does not mean that you will definitely have a difficult life but it means that the odds are stacked against you from the very beginning. As I have stated previously, you have to play the odds. Successful people build a solid foundation of self, career, marriage, and home before they have children.

Disclaimer: there are a plethora of child-raising/psychology books out there by people who have dedicated their entire life to developing an expertise in this area. Below, I address some real-world issues in as candid and direct a way as possible based on my personal experience as a father.

Use Birth Control

As with many parents, public health experts, therapists, teachers, and thousands of professionals who care about our society, I find it tremendously frustrating to witness how people who can access good information about sexual health fail to use birth control when they have sex. It is an enduring truth rooted in the power of the sex drive: if you have unprotected sex, you are likely to become or get someone pregnant. That's all there is to it. It is far too late in our society's development to ignore this important fact. If you are not smart enough to use birth control, you certainly are not smart enough to have children. The best way to prevent unwanted pregnancies is to practice abstinence. If you are not going to practice abstinence, then you and your partner must use birth control to prevent unwanted pregnancies and the spread of sexually transmitted diseases. It is that simple.

Please do not let a few minutes of ecstasy turn your life into agony.

It Is Fine Not to Have Kids

Why do you want to have children? This is the question each person should ask him or herself.

The reality is that too many people have children simply because they feel like that is what women, or married people, are supposed to do. You need to make sure that you are in a position to have children, though. In addition to the pure desire to bring a child into the world, you also need both the time and money.

Note for couples with two demanding careers: if one of you does not lessen the value of your career, you will feel increased time stress by having to juggle full-time careers and children. This could lead to marital problems or even divorce if you don't work out a new way of organizing your life. Children are more demanding than you realize and you cannot control them like you can certain aspects of your career. Be honest with yourself about your personal needs and know that it is perfectly fine not to have children. If you already have children, we advise you to pay more attention to the choices you and your partner are making about time, money, and parenting. Are you stretched too thin? Are you struggling to keep up with your role in your kids' lives?

Do You Have the Time?

This is a simple question that is not always answered before having children. You must be able to answer these questions before you think about having a child:

- Is someone going to stay home with your child?
- If so, for how long?
- If not, who will take off from work when your child is sick?
- Who will get your child ready and drop him off at the caregiver in the morning?
- Who will pick your child up on time after work?
- Who will get your child to her extracurricular activities?
- Who is responsible for helping your child with his homework?

There are many questions and situations that can be anticipated before you embark on parenthood. Ask the difficult questions beforehand and make sure you have all of the answers before you bring a child into the picture.

Do You Have the Money?

Why is it that you cannot buy a car or a house unless you have the proper level of money or credit, but you can have a child whenever you want? Of course, people fall in love and want to have children. But you must understand that children are expensive and in the economic environment we live in, you must be prepared for this reality. There are many expenses that can be anticipated when having a child but there are also many that cannot. Are you financially secure enough to provide for your children? You need to answer questions in the affirmative, such as:

- Can we sacrifice one income to stay at home?
- If so, for how long?
- Can we afford daycare or a nanny?
- Is our home appropriate for children?
- Are we in a position to save for college?
- Is the primary income stable enough to cover the additional financial stress of a child while sacrificing the other career?

A good exercise is to use the budget worksheet in chapter 4 to perform a "what if" scenario so you can see how to make the financial sacrifices work for you. If it does not work on paper, it will *not* work in the real world. Make sure that you can exist in the real world financially with a nest egg built up before you even start considering having a child.

Don't Have Them Too Early

In my survey of financially successful people, one of the interesting items that popped up was that the average age of couples having their first child was twenty-eight (I would expect this to be even higher in major metropolitan areas and for people whose careers take longer to become established, such as doctors). This makes sense because in your twenties you need to work hard to establish your career. Then you get married. It takes time to work out differences and establish a good compatible relationship. Only then can you think about children. It is very difficult to do all of that and have children much sooner. If you have children in your early twenties, you will have a difficult time financially because you will have additional expenses and it will be more difficult to dedicate the necessary time to advance your career. Therefore, don't be in a rush.

Once You Have Children, You Are Never Divorced

A marriage becomes permanent when you have children. Sure, you can legally become divorced but you are *never* permanently separated. The reason you got divorced is likely due to an inability to compromise or irreconcilable differences. Divorce, when you have children, only makes this problem worse, however. Think of things like:

- How are you going to share custody?
- How are you going to afford living in two locations?
- How are you going to interact at your children's events (school, graduation, weddings, or when your children start having children)?

You can see that although you can divorce your spouse, you will always have to deal with your ex. I am not sure there is a more difficult situation in existence than having to negotiate with an angry ex about your mutual children's lives.

If your relationship is not rock solid, do *not* have children.

Your Children Will Not Be Perfect. Can You Handle That?

One of the most interesting things I have learned by having my own children is that every child has her or his own personality that is very evident from the earliest years. I always thought a child's behavior and personality was based on how he or she was raised. Good parents can have bad kids and bad parents can have good kids. It is an odd fact of life.

If you don't feel you can handle having a difficult or "imperfect" child, do not have children.

Make Sure You Are Stable before You Have Children

Psychological issues and diseases seem more prevalent today than ever before. If you, or your spouse, has an instable mental or emotional state, let this be a major warning sign for you. You should seriously consider not having children if this is the case. Children cause great stress and you may not be able to handle that extra stress in your life if you are already trying to make yourself better. Additionally, many problems of this nature are genetic. If you are suffering from a mental illness, there is a good chance that your child will develop the same problem. That will make raising them more stressful as well.

Children Don't Always Listen and You Can't Fire Them

Your children will not listen to you all the time, no matter how much you'd like to think they will. Children have their own thoughts and also test their independence (much earlier than you might think!). Many parents who have strong careers or are perfectionists have trouble granting their children the room to make minor bad decisions. These same parents also become frustrated when their children do not respond to them the same way their employees at the office do.

Make sure you have the necessary patience before you have children.

Children Become More Expensive as They Grow Older

I used to think that the most expensive stage for children was before they entered school. At that time, I was paying a lot for proper care for my children while my wife and I were at work. As my children have gotten older and I have gotten to know people with children older than mine, I realize that preschool-aged children were *not* the most expensive. As children grow older, their clothes, hobbies, and activities become more expensive. Then when they start to drive, many children expect their parents to help them buy a car, pay for insurance, and help maintain the vehicle. Then it is time for college. After that, it is time to throw the wedding of your daughter's dreams. There may also be additional expenses, especially if your child has any financial problems (due to college loans, a lost job, etc.) and she needs to borrow money from you.

Another factor that makes children expensive is that they have such easy access through the media (television and Internet) to see what other children are acquiring from their parents. These unrealistic expectations can cause a tremendous amount of stress in the relationship between parents and children—and on your wallet.

What If You Have Children before You Are Ready?

I hope you have a supportive family because you will need them! This is a time to get rid of your ego and accept all of the help anyone offers. This is going to be a challenging time, not only for you, but also for those who are helping because they are sacrificing things as well.

It is important to understand that having one child will make your life very difficult but manageable. The effect of any more children will likely be catastrophic and permanent.

Observations for Those Who Want Children

Now that you have decided to have children, there are a few things you need to know that will help you survive this life change. First and foremost, your children must become your number one priority for their first eighteen years (and possibly more) of life. This requires sacrifices in many areas including personal, career, and your marriage. Children put unforeseen stresses on your marriage, making your partnership lack any sort of "fun" at any given point. You will need to work through these tough times to avoid divorce. The rewards of doing so will be great because they will strengthen your bond with your spouse.

Below are various observations that will help you as you enter this challenging, demanding, and incredibly rewarding phase of your life.

Children Come Out with a Personality

When my wife was carrying our first child, he moved around a little in the womb but was relatively calm. When he was born, he was a mellow child who was not in a rush to do anything early and he loved being pampered. He was exactly what an infant was supposed to be in my mind and a true joy.

Then our second child came. Before he was even born, he was sparring in the womb. When he was an infant he would fuss all the time and did not enjoy cuddling as much as his old brother had. At two years old, he was kicked out of daycare for pulling the fire alarm, biting, and other "naughty" things. We felt absolutely horrible and thought we were bad parents. One of the owners of the daycare said that although my son couldn't stay, his activity showed that he was going to be a very verbal child and he was demonstrating a lot of curiosity coupled with frustration. She was absolutely correct. Once he could verbally communicate, he settled down because he could say what he wanted. He also has a very active imagination that cracks us up on a daily basis. When you have children, be ready because it is like rolling dice on how they come out.

Two Is More than Twice the Work

With one child, you have double coverage. It is wonderful to come home from work and want to spend some time with your child and give your spouse a break.

With two children, you have man-to-man coverage. When you walk in the door after a long workday, you are not asked whether you want to spend time with your child—the question is which one do you want to deal with. No one gets a break. And when they get older, you and your spouse are required to drive them to all of their activities (which always seem to overlap).

With three (or more!) children, you have to drop back into zone coverage. This causes you to have exponentially more demands with virtually no time for yourself so you can "recharge your batteries." It requires a special person to thrive in this chaotic home environment.

Avoid Giving Your Children Names That You Would Not Want for Yourself

It drives me crazy when parents give their children ridiculous names. I know there is usually the best of intentions behind these decisions, but many parents don't see the situation from the child's point of view as they grow up. I know a young child with the name Infinity. Every single time she is introduced to a new person, an awkward moment ensues as the adult tries to figure out her name and how it is spelled. There are a few important points to keep in mind when choosing names for your children:

- If the average person can't spell it, don't use it.
- Don't tweak the traditional spelling.
- Don't name your child something and then expect everyone to pronounce his or her name in some fancy way.
- Do the rhyme game—make sure your child's name does not rhyme with something that will torment him or her on the playground.
- You don't need to continue a family tradition that has been established by handing down a goofy family name for the future generations.

- Name them something that will work when they get older. (Note: I dislike my name but I also cannot figure out how to change it, so I am stuck!)

Agree with Your Spouse in front of Your Children

Children are excellent at splitting you and your spouse apart. They will always ask one parent for something if they decide they have the highest probability of getting the answer they want from that parent. If they do not receive the desired answer, they will ask the other parent. This will become a lifelong hassle if you give a different answer than your spouse.

Always agree in front of your children with your spouse's decision. If you do not agree, then go behind closed doors to discuss. If you decide as a team on a different decision, then let the spouse who made the original decision state the new decision.

Another approach is to discuss the decision with your spouse and the child at the same time, prior to making a decision. All information shared will be consistent and a good decision can hopefully be made. This will help your child learn good conflict-resolution and decision-making skills. Children need to know that your relationship is strong and that they cannot manipulate you or pin one parent against the other.

Take a Vacation from Your Children

Many people feel guilty about leaving their children behind when they take a vacation. Fortunately, my wife and I have gotten over this. Your children can become the center of your universe and make your relationship with your spouse suffer. Don't let this happen. Make sure that you find time for the two of you. It can be a date night, a weekend away, or even a longer vacation. A strong relationship is the most important determinant in a happy home for your children to be raised in. Your children will survive without you. In fact, it is good for them to learn that they will be fine without you.

Other Children Can Scream in My Ears

Before I had children of my own, all kids used to drive me crazy when they misbehaved. If I was on a plane, it seemed I always got the seat in front of a three-year-old who would kick the back of my seat and scream in my ear for the entire flight. I would flash the mom dirty looks to try and shame her into getting her child under control. I used to think that if I had children, they would *never* behave this way on a plane, in a store, or anywhere else in public.

Then I had my own children. They did all the things on a plane that I used to hate. I tried like crazy to get them to stop but sometimes there was nothing I could do.

Now when I am on a plane, other people's children don't bother me. I don't hear the screaming and I don't feel the kicking of my seat. It still surprises me. I share a common experience of parenthood with those parents. I am glad my children are no longer at that stage and appreciate how the parents are doing the best they can in a stressful situation.

Children teach us patience and tolerance.

Your Child Won't Be a Professional Athlete, So Calm Down

I was in professional sports for several years and here is what I learned: Your child needs (1) the physical ability, (2) the smarts, and (3) the heart to be a professional athlete. Professional athletes are physically gifted and have a true passion for their sport. Genetics also plays a large part in determining whether a child will become a professional athlete.

That being said, your child's chance of becoming a professional athlete is remote. Even if your son or daughter does make it that far, there are actually very few athletes who make a good enough living (and save enough) to continue that lifestyle for the rest of their lives. Youth sports is primarily about learning life lessons, such as how to function in a team environment, operate within a set of rules, and handle winning and losing. It is not about reliving your high school days when you were a frustrated athlete. As your child plays a sport and improves, you need to help him find his passion. That comes from quiet encouragement, and not yelling and acting like a knucklehead in the stands.

Keep in mind that when you yell at the players, coach, or referee, you are probably proving that you are an idiot. I would suggest that you remain quiet and keep that fact a secret.

Let Your Children Know That They Must Continually Earn Your Trust

Trust is earned, not given. Also, as a parent, your job is to keep your children safe and to nurture them, not be their best friend. Children—especially very young children—do not have enough experience to make good decisions all of the time. They need their parents' help to stay on the right course, particularly during the challenging teenage years.

I have made it clear to my boys that they are not "given" trust. They must continually earn my trust. In fact, it takes a lifetime to earn my trust and only a moment to lose it. My children are in a more difficult situation than most because both parents started their careers as auditors. I've told them that as long as they live under my roof, they are subject to periodic, surprise "audits." This is for their safety, of course. I want them to know this at a young age so that they will not be surprised when punishment is doled out. If it is always a rule, then they can't get mad (well, not too mad).

Set the proper expectations with your children before trust becomes an issue.

Create an Environment for Candid Discussions

Do you think your children are going to do anything different from you as a child? No. In fact, your children will likely be more curious because they are exposed to so much more through the media and the Internet. Be honest with your children and help them to understand the importance of making good decisions. You can only shelter them for so long. They will have questions, and if you are not answering them honestly, someone else will and you may lose your children's trust in the process.

It is key that your children understand the importance of making good decisions, so teach them through conversation and good examples.

Why Do We Teach Our Children "the Fairy Tale"?

I fail to understand why some parents ingrain "the fairy tale" into their children about meeting a prince or princess and living happily ever after. Later in my chapter about happiness, I demonstrate how setting a reasonable level of expectations will lead to happiness. If we set our expectations too high, we will be chronically disappointed. Therefore, why would we want to ingrain a view of reality in our children that is at the highest expectation level possible?

At some point your child will find out that this fairy tale is not true and he or she may become very upset. If this realization happens during the teenage years, your son or daughter may start making a lot of bad decisions because they will feel ready to rebel against your high expectations. If they don't find out until after they are married, your son or daughter may find him or herself in a miserable marriage and may divorce at a later date. Either way, the deck is stacked against them if they aren't grounded in reality.

Be honest with your child and tell her that she needs to work hard, make good decisions, and be in control of her own destiny. Parents also need to prepare their sons for a more active role in caretaking than historically expected of men, as we've highlighted previously about male Caretakers.

Homeschooling—Great in Theory, Not So Much in Reality

I have had the opportunity to meet several people who homeschool their children. Homeschooling is a fantastic idea in theory because the children get more individual attention than in a regular classroom and their curriculum can be customized to meet the needs of each child. You can also shelter your children from some of the negative influences they may be exposed to at a public or private school.

Unfortunately, I have met very few families who homeschool their children and who lead relatively normal social lives. In reality, here are the problems with homeschooling:

- Homeschooling parents may have social anxiety themselves that they are projecting onto their children. Encourage someone you know with this problem to get family counseling. Homeschooled kids are already at risk of being isolated from their peers. The lack of social interaction and experience when a child is homeschooled will greatly handicap your child as he emerges into high school or college.
- These parents prevent their children from seeing and experiencing the real world. The longer your children go without existing in the real world, the harder it will be for them to adapt.
- The homeschool curriculum will likely exclude controversial topics and provide a narrower perspective on life.
- Homeschooled children will be limited by the intelligence and skills of their parents.
- Academics are only half of a proper education. The other half is developing strong social skills. Many homeschooled children have heavily underdeveloped social skills.

Children Need to Be Involved in Various Activities

If you are going to have children, they need to be involved in various extracurricular activities. Being exposed to various activities will help your children find their passions, understand what they are good at, and become more well-rounded individuals.

Another important benefit of exposing your children to new activities is that they will establish different groups of friends. Children will fall out of favor with a group of friends at some point during their young lives. It is important that they have another positive group to shift to while time heals the problems with the first group. If they do not have a positive group to shift to, your child could fall into a group of negative friends who are always looking to pull people down to their level. Once involved with a negative group, it is often difficult for a child to leave.

A special note for those parents who tend to go overboard with after-school activities: Allow your children to have time with no activities as well. This will allow them the opportunity to build their creativity, hone their imagination, and simply enjoy being a child.

When You Are Done Having Children, Consider Getting Fixed

Some friends of ours have a child that is the same age as our youngest. One summer when our friends' child was in first grade, they announced they were pregnant. Within twenty-four hours of hearing the news, I had scheduled my vasectomy.

I have thoroughly enjoyed my children but it is also nice as they progress from one stage to the next. Each stage seems to give them a little more independence, which results in a higher level of freedom for the parents as well. As a parent, it has been liberating for me to emerge from the stages of constantly monitoring every move by our children as they become less and less dependent.

Having another child after achieving a certain level of freedom can be difficult to adjust to. That is why you can use the conveniences of modern medicine to ensure that does not happen to you.

Teenagers Need Jobs

When I was thirteen, my dad dragged me out to the golf course and had me caddie for him and his buddy. I remember getting to the par four, eighteenth hole. After carrying two bags for seventeen holes, the eighteenth hole looked like it was two miles long. I finally made it to the green. When everyone putted out and finished the round, it came time to pay me. Both my dad and his friend slapped $12 in my hand and it was the best feeling I had ever had. Needless to say, I was ready to go again!

When I got home, I was fired up because I was thinking of all the things I was going to buy with the money I earned. It was at that point that I realized $24 did not go very far. I also realized that as great as $6 an hour was, it was not nearly enough. I then learned that in order to get paid more, I needed to have a better education.

Teenagers need to learn the value of money, how to earn it, and how to manage their spending. How can they do that if they don't have a job? Encourage your teenage child to apply and take various jobs that will give them a sense of accomplishment, independence, and financial freedom.

Cars for Teenagers

Let's all make a pact right now that, as parents, we will stop buying our children nice cars. There are so many reasons we need to be careful:

- Providing a new vehicle for your child raises their expectations for the rest of their lives—and can be devastating when they cannot afford that new car down the road.
- This type of purchase can put your family under additional financial stress.
- A car that is too fast will cause safety concerns.
- How responsible is your child? How can you be sure they are not drinking, drugging, or texting while driving?

At an age when teenagers tend to believe they are bulletproof, one bad decision in a car can change someone's life forever (or end it!). You need to make sure that your children are as educated as possible when they start driving. Then you need to continually monitor their ability to use this privilege responsibly.

I have also told my children that I will help them get their first car by paying for half of a rust-colored 1983 Toyota Tercel hatchback with 100 percent "pleather" seats, just like I had.

College or a Job . . . Just Ask My Kids

One of the best things my parents did was to help me understand that when I graduated from high school, I was gone. They told me they would pay for college and they convinced me that it was the only way to afford the kind of lifestyle I wanted to have. That is why education was so important. They also told me I only had four years to complete my education. This taught me to buckle down and study hard so I could guarantee a four-year college degree.

Many people do not grow up with that strong understanding of the importance of a good education. Parents then complain because they can't get their children "off the payroll." That is why my children already know that they are gone after high school. College is the best option, but if they don't pursue that, then they have to get a job. Living at home is not an option past the time they receive their high school diploma.

The military or learning a trade is a great option for teenagers who are not sure that college is right for them. The military experience will help your child mature *and* it will help pay for college if they choose to attend. Learning a trade is valuable because skilled labor will always be needed. This is also a good way to be self-employed or own a company in the future.

What Does It Take to Get into College?

College is very important for your child in order to expedite his or her ability to get on solid financial ground when he or she gets older. Therefore, it is important for you to know what is expected of your child to facilitate his or her process of being admitted. The following are a few tips to facilitate the college application process:

- Save money for college.
- Strive for a high grade point average (GPA).
- Take the SATs (and ACTs where applicable) a few times and focus on specific study courses and guides to prepare for these tests.
- Have a job.
- Perform community service.
- Be involved in at least one sport or activity.
- Have a leadership role in your job, community service, sport, or other activity.
- Complete the college application accurately.
- Submit the application early to give yourself the best odds and as many options as possible.

- Emphasize any minority group of which you are a part (it helps).
- Find well-respected alumnus of target colleges who can write letters of recommendation for you.

You need to help your child "build his résumé" to maximize his chances of getting into a good school. Understanding this process will help him when it is time for him to apply for a real job as well.

Let Children Go When They Are Ready

You must allow your children enough room to make their own mistakes as they mature. Eventually, you need to let them go completely so they can discover the world on their own. Many parents smother their children and do not allow them this opportunity for selfish reasons.

You must not let your loneliness be the reason that you stunt the growth opportunities of your children.

Parents Who Bought This Book for Their Child

If you bought this book for your child, you should read it first and highlight the areas you feel are most important, add comments that are important to you that may not be included, and cross out any advice you do not agree with. Then, to help your child understand that you are serious about the information provided, I have enclosed a contract for you on the next page. This will help your child understand that when he or she becomes a teenager, it is time to start taking responsibility for his or her life. Your son or daughter needs to understand the importance of working hard and making good decisions. This book is an excellent tool for your child to use as part of this process. Also, by having your teenage child read and keep a copy of this book with your notes, you will have documentation that you gave them good advice prior to him or her making bad decisions he or she may possibly make.

CONTRACT

This contract is between _____
("Parent(s)") and _____ ("Child") and
has been entered into on _____ (Date).
This contract acknowledges that Parent(s) have read this book and
have made the necessary notes on relevant pages to ensure that their
views and advice are properly included and emphasized. Child
acknowledges receipt of this book on the date stated above and the
contents therein. Child agrees to read this book and ask questions
as they arise. Child also agrees to keep this book for reference
purposes so that guidance can be gained for future situations that
have not been contemplated by Child as of this date. Child also
acknowledges that the key to a successful and fulfilling life is to:

1. Work hard.
2. Make good decisions.
3. Open each element of life in order and only after the prior
    element has been mastered.

Bad decisions from this day forward that have been covered in this
book or additional comments by Parent(s) are the responsibility of
Child. Child cannot blame or otherwise hold Parent(s) responsible
for decisions made by Child.

Signed and acknowledged by:

_____   _____

(Parent 1)   (Parent 2, if applicable)

_____

(Child)

Summary

Remember that it is totally acceptable *not* to have children. Even if you want children, you do not necessarily need to have them at this very moment. It is best to work hard to build a strong foundation (financially and with your relationship) that will help you focus on being the best parent you can be. You will know you are at this point when you have the desire, time, *and* money to think about raising a child.

Now that we have covered the last element of life, it is time for a quick, fun chapter. Pets are a relatively minor part of the big life picture and not worthy of its own element in the matrix of life. Unfortunately, though, too many people make mistakes when it comes to the timing of when to get a pet (me included!), that I feel it is important to address it briefly in the following pages.

Chapter 11:
Pets

Even though the subject of pet ownership does not warrant a larger discussion, the timing as to when to adopt a pet is a common error that many people make. Many people grow up with pets and feel the need to continue that companionship when they move away from their parents and enter the real world. You should put this need into perspective, however. Owning a pet is an important life lesson that teaches caring and sensitivity early in life. When you move out of your parents' house, you need to focus on college and then on starting your career. This is a very exciting time but also extremely unpredictable. Pets will hinder your need for flexibility greatly because you will be worrying about walking, feeding, and giving them attention on a daily basis. You will also find yourself in a tight financial situation when you first start your career since the incremental costs of a pet (food, supplies, boarding, and veterinary visits) may cause money problems.

The problems with having a pet when you first live on your own include:

- Pets take time. Your focus needs to be on your career when you complete school. A good start to your career will catapult you ahead of your peers. You do not want the distraction and regimented schedule required by a pet at this point in time. Can you imagine not being able to work on an important, high-exposure project because you need to let your dog out?
- You may meet someone who has some type of issue with the pet you have (i.e., allergies, phobias, or general dislike).

- A pet can also cause problems with your housing situation. At this point in your life, you should be renting because you need to stay agile and minimize outside distractions. Many apartment complexes will not allow pets or have severe restrictions or high pet deposits.
- Pets often have many hidden costs that are not contemplated at the time people adopt them, like food, supplies, veterinarian visits, annual shot requirements, preventive medicines, and boarding when you go on vacation.
- Pets, especially puppies, can destroy your furniture and other home possessions.
- Pets can be protective and may cause problems when friends come to visit.

For people entering the real world, your desire to have a pet is adolescent. For those who are past the point of having children or their children have left the house, a pet can be a great companion that can help prevent your feeling lonely or inactive.

My Naïve Experience with a Dog

When I was twenty-two, I rented a house with two friends. We had jobs that required we put in more than forty hours per week quite frequently. We also had very active social lives, to say the least. One of my roommates decided that we had a perfect house for a dog, so we went to the shelter and adopted a beautiful husky mix. He was awesome!

We had fun with him over the weekend around the house but then we went back to work on Monday. By Friday, we were arguing so badly about who was going to be home in time to let him out and feed him that we realized we were not in the right situation to properly care for him. We also had sufficient time to realize that he had one annoying problem—he humped everyone!

On Saturday, he went back to the shelter. It was simply not the right time in my life to have a pet.

My Naïve Experience with a Cat

A few years later, when I moved in with my wife, we bought a Persian cat because she had always wanted one. We named him Max after the Grinch's dog and he was a great cat (I can't believe I paid $450 for a cat when you can get them for free at a shelter!). He was a purebred with a beautiful gray coat of long hair and piercing blue eyes. His best characteristic was that he had the personality of a dog. When we brought him home he was so tiny that he looked like a dust bunny with four Q-Tips sticking out of his body. He was so small (and unathletic) that we had to make steps out of some pillows that he could use to get on and off our bed.

Max was the focus of our time whenever we were home. A few years later, we had our first son. Our son then became the primary focus of our lives because newborns require constant attention. Max was not a big fan of our son, to say the least.

I discovered how Max's dissatisfaction with the situation manifested itself when I walked through the living room one day and there was an unfamiliar odor in the air. I sniffed around the room like a dog. I finally discovered the source of the foul odor. We had drapes that "puddled" on the floor and Max had decided to urinate behind this puddle! When I pulled the drapes back I unleashed a stench that I had never smelled before. Luckily, we were able to cut off the excess fabric on the drapes and re-hem them to fix the problem . . . or so we thought.

Max then found a new spot to pee, and another, and another. We replaced our carpet several times and even moved once. In our new house, Max took a liking to the dining room. I built a fence around the dining room to stop him from urinating there because nothing else was working. After that, Max just found a new spot in the living room. I finally had enough!

My wife went out of town with our boys (we had our second son in the meantime) and I told her that Max would not be there when she returned. In our relationship, I take care of many of the difficult situations and my wife pretends like it never happened to this day.

I tried to take Max to the shelter and they would not take him because he was too old. My last resort was to take him to the vet and have him put to sleep. When I arrived, they asked why I was putting him down. I felt like "peeing all over the house" was not a good reason, so I said that my youngest son was severely allergic to him. He was out of town and I had to have Max out before he came back.

The veterinarian's assistant said she knew of an older lady who loved these kinds of cats and had several. She asked if I would mind giving Max to her. I was ecstatic that I did not have to put him to sleep, and so was my wife. And the whole family enjoyed an odor-free home for many years to come.

The Right Time to Get a Pet

When my sons got a little older (and were out of diapers!), we got them two dogs. Everyone knows their spot in the pecking order, so it has worked out great.

You have plenty of time to have pets in your life. Wait for a time when you are in a stable situation so your pets can live their whole, happy lives with you.

PART III

WHAT GIVES OUR LIVES DEPTH

The next section of this book explains what gives our lives depth. These factors are:

- Happiness
- Financial Success
- Achievement

So far, we have learned about the foundation (three primary sources of stress) and structure (core components of life) of our modern society. The key to life is adding depth. The following two chapters address the determining factors of depth.

There will be times in your life that short-term sacrifices of happiness will be required to provide financial success and achievements. Financial success and achievements will then fuel future levels of happiness. We call this the Happiness/Success Dilemma, illustrated here:

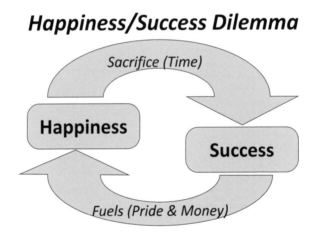

Happiness/Success Dilemma

There is no right or wrong answer as to how we should manage this dilemma. Understanding it and how we react to it, though, will help us set our goals and expectations at the appropriate level. In turn, this will help us maximize our time. The process of managing this dilemma is what causes each of us to be different at the very core of our being.

Once the elements that give our lives depth are addressed, we will then move on to the final chapter, where we bring together all the components of this book, on which you will be able to build your own personalized matrix of life.

CHAPTER 12: HAPPINESS

Happiness is essential to our culture, so much so that our Founding Fathers started the Preamble to the Declaration of Independence by stating, "We hold these Truths to be self-evident, that all Men are created equal, that they are endowed, by their Creator, with certain unalienable Rights, that among these are Life, Liberty and the *Pursuit of Happiness* [emphasis mine]." Happiness is defined as consistently meeting or exceeding your expectations. In this chapter you will learn:

- Where happiness comes from
- How to set reasonable expectations
- How to find your passion
- How happiness changes over time
- How to recognize your spirituality and purpose

A great anecdote for personal expectations happened one day while I was working for Price Waterhouse on one of our largest clients. My boss was extremely well respected by everyone in the firm, as well as the client. He and I were talking, and he asked me, "Do you know what the problem is with our society?" This piqued my curiosity into this pearl of wisdom, so I asked him what it was. He stated that the problem was that people set their expectations too high. He said, "Everyone wants to be CEO of a large company. Everyone should actually set their expectations to arrive at work safely. That way, once they get to work safely, they are having a great day!"

There is usually some truth in each joke. In this case, there is a lot of truth. *The more reasonably you set your expectations, the happier you will be.* The main drivers of expectations include, but are not limited to:

- Positive attitude
- Safety and security
- Good health
- Laughter
- Personal relationships
- Hobbies and other personal interests
- Travel
- Spiritual growth
- Openness to differences of opinion

It is important for you to understand what makes you happy so that you can then appropriately set your expectations. Expectations are generally more static and must be achieved on a regular, almost daily, basis for you to be happy. Some of your expectations will change over time as you open more core components of life. Therefore, a solid foundation needs to be built at each stage of your life so that happiness can be achieved in the future as well.

General Advice and Observations

Many people expect others to bring them happiness, whether they are parents, friends, or companions, but the reality is that no one can *make* you happy. Happiness is a feeling that you create with your connection to that person's energy. You decide if the presence or absence of that person's energy gives you a good feeling or not. Thus, you make yourself happy when you are in the presence of that person. Happiness can be enhanced by certain relationships but the source of all happiness comes from within.

Happiness is also a choice. Understanding who you are and what is important to you is essential for you to achieve happiness on a consistent basis. People may have similar definitions of happiness but no two people will have the exact same definition.

What makes each of us happy is as unique as a fingerprint.

Set Reasonable Expectations

As previously discussed, you must set reasonable expectations. The evidence of your ability to set reasonable expectations is that you should be meeting them on a regular basis—daily for some. If you are not, you have likely set your expectations too high or you are in a situation that is preventing you from achieving what you desire.

Be flexible with your expectations as well. Your definition of "fun" will change over time, and you must allow your expectations to adapt to the changes in your life. Dramatic changes can occur when your career changes, you get married, you buy a home, or when you have children. As a result, what makes you happy will change as well. Your expectations need to be updated as your life changes.

Be Honest with Who You Are

The major cause of social unhappiness is not being honest with who you are. Use the 1–10 scale when assessing situations, with 1 being the lowest and 10 being the highest. For example, I rate myself as an 8 in golf. When playing against people who are at my same level or slightly better, I have a blast! When I play with people much worse than I, I do not feel challenged and become slightly bored. When I play with people much better than I, I know that they are not challenged and are not enjoying the experience as much as if they were playing with a better golfer. No matter the situation, you must find an area in which you can connect on a similar level with another person (or people). Is it intellectual, humor, physical appearance, personality, athletic ability, career, common interests, heritage, or spirituality? If you cannot find the common ground, do not become disappointed when no connection is made.

Be Ruthless in Self-examination

As a former Bank of America employee, Vernon is a big fan of the bank's former leader, Hugh McColl, for his folksy charm and Southern directness. In a recent interview, Hugh McColl invoked an old saying that Vernon believes is a great definition for happiness: "It's been said that the definition of happiness is when a person makes peace between his ambitions and his limitations." Vernon loves this definition of happiness simply because it involves being present in and introspective of your own life. This requires that you step back and think about how well you are suited to accomplish your goals. Being brutally honest with assessing where you are today is the first step. It is simply an acknowledgment of the situation that you find yourself in today. While it is important to step back and think about the decisions that helped you reach this point in your life, don't beat yourself up over them. Acknowledge them, understand the consequences, and move forward. Lying to yourself about your current situation will affect your ability to meet your expectations and thus impede your happiness.

Happiness Must Come from Making Good Decisions

Happiness must come from positive sources. As Vernon mentioned earlier, some people make very poor decisions in the name of achieving happiness. Generally, these bad decisions come from trying to *avoid* a period of being unhappy. Happiness should never be derived from doing anything illegal or anything that hurts other people.

Jails are full of people who missed this lesson growing up!

Savor the Simple Things

As your life becomes more complicated and your definition of "fun" changes, you can lose sight of some of those simple things that make you happy. The simple things that make me happy usually remind me of things I enjoyed at a simpler time. They include:

- Playing a round of golf at Canoe Brook Country Club in Summit, New Jersey
- Eating a Dagwood sandwich at the Avenue Deli in New Providence, New Jersey, or a slice of pizza at Pete's Pizzeria in Morristown, New Jersey
- Listening to "Take Me Home Country Roads," which reminds me of the summers I spent at the Jersey shore
- Drinking some Brunnelo di Montalcino, which reminds me of a fantastic vacation I spent in a villa in Tuscany with my wife and some great friends
- Walking around the campus of Wake Forest University
- Attending Opening Day at Rangers Ballpark in Arlington (the most pure, pageantry-filled day in professional baseball)

I enjoy playing golf but when I play it too much, it is no longer special to me. Be sure not to overuse the simple things so that they will remain special and will continue to be a source of happiness for you.

Maintain Your Energy

Your energy level is one of the most important measures of your level of happiness. When you are running on positive energy, you will create even more happiness for yourself, and it can be contagious to those around you as well. This energy has both a physical and emotional aspect. As you mature and advance through life, you will develop an understanding of activities or work that add to your energy, and those that take away from it. Please understand the important difference between choices that generally bring you happiness, such as a good marriage or a career that suits you well, and daily activities or choices that drain your energy. It is difficult to be happy while performing daily energy-killing activities. For example, you may love your job but discover that skipping your workouts or time with friends in service of the job begins to wear away at your well-being. You may have a great spouse or relationship, but if your personality is sustained and energized by "alone time"—reading, praying, or walking—being a couple constantly on the move may ultimately become self-defeating.

If your current job is not one that provides you with energy, you have several choices to make:

1. You can carve out time to do simple things that provide you energy outside of work.
2. You should make an effort to find the things about your job that you enjoy and focus on those. Also, realize that the other tasks you do on the job provide the fuel for creating the life you want.
3. You can always interview for a different job. You will either find a better one or realize that what you have is actually not so bad.

You can feel overwhelmed if your batteries aren't recharged on a regular basis.

Find Your Passion

What is your passion? It can be anything, really, but you need to be sure it is positive. A few examples include working out, spending quality time with a special person, being a great parent, coaching, helping others, making money, playing a sport, or socializing. Your passion does not have to be limited to one area but rather it can encompass several.

There will be times in your life when you are led away from your passion(s). These are usually times of great change in your life. At these times, you need to dedicate your time to mastering a new challenge (such as a promotion, getting married, or having a child). Upon mastering the challenge, you must take a step back and see whether that challenge has caused you to change your passion(s). Having children is the most common factor that can change your passion(s).

Passions also take time and usually require some money. As your life becomes more complicated, both of these areas will turn out to be more constrained. You will need to balance the new demands on your time and money with your passion. This is one of the most difficult challenges as your life becomes more complicated.

Who You Surround Yourself with Directly Impacts Your Happiness

We all know a few people who seem to be able to suck the life out of even the best party. How do you handle those people when they enter your life? Do you feel guilty about avoiding them? Most people do. It is essential that you do your best to avoid them, however cold and callous that may sound. But if people do not want to help themselves, there is virtually nothing you can do. When amateurs try to save a drowning person, usually the drowning person grabs on to the person trying to save them and they both drown.

This is a major issue for young adults. When we are at that stage of life, we start making most of our own decisions. This is an extremely important part of preparing ourselves for the real world. Unfortunately, we usually do not fully understand the relevance and impact of our decisions when we start making them on our own. It is only after a few years, and a lot of experience, that we understand why some decisions are good and some are not. One of the most significant decisions we make is with whom we surround ourselves. The better choices we make, the happier we will be in the long term, even though it may not seem like it at the time.

You must surround yourself with positive people who respect what makes you happy, who encourage your personal growth, and who enable you to meet your expectations.

Sometimes You Must Sacrifice Happiness

I have addressed how important happiness is but happiness must not be your sole driver. As addressed earlier, I call this the Happiness/Success Dilemma. You will need to sacrifice happiness at times to achieve success that will then fuel your pride and provide money to finance your lifestyle. Your pride in the future will be based on your achievements (as a spouse, as a parent, and as a member of your community). Additionally, money does not make you happy, but the *lack* of money will make your life very difficult. Happiness gets more expensive as you get older—it's a truism. This happens for a couple reasons. First, you will continually want to experience more than what you have previously done. Second, inflation will make the same standard of living more expensive in the future. A few example of sacrifice are:

- As a student, good grades are an incredibly important focus. Good grades are the foundation that the rest of your life is based upon. Students who have fun first and receive lower grades in the process limit their future potential significantly.
- When in your twenties, advancing your career is essential. You must be willing to work more than forty hours per week at times. Those who jump out to an early lead in their careers have a distinct advantage for the next forty years in the workforce.
- Upon getting married, you truly learn what the word *compromise* means. As a couple, you will need to make certain sacrifices so that you and your partner can merge your lives together. No two people are exactly the same. Without compromise, your marriage will not last.
- Having children will have the single largest impact on your happiness. Children take time, money, and

responsibility. A fragile new life now depends on you. Young children also demand your constant attention. This time drain will impact your level of happiness because you will simply not have the time to do many of the things that used to make you happy. This is the type of sacrifice that will help your life be much more fulfilling over time. And as you spend more and more time with your children, you will find that your areas of happiness will change and become more focused on your kids.

It's about Perspective

Having laid out my Success/Happiness Dilemma for you, Vernon wants you to consider this: "Enjoy the journey. While I didn't love graduate school, I learned to love and appreciate what it was giving me. While I don't necessarily enjoy running, I learned to enjoy and appreciate the benefits. While sitting still and reading is difficult for me, I absolutely love the knowledge and perspective that I gain. Any perceivably mundane activity seems useless without a grander purpose. It's critical to understand that purpose and make connections for everything that you do. I like to think about this as a different degree of happiness. The happiness should come from the knowledge that you are moving in the right direction. In essence, it's having faith in yourself."

Purpose Makes It Easier

My personal view of spirituality is that it is the gift wrap that holds a life together. When I write spirituality, I don't want you to confuse it with religion. While religion may be an aspect of how one demonstrates spirituality, I want you to think in much broader terms.

Inside of each of us resides a light that was put there by our creator. I envision this as a pure energy encased in a glass sphere. This inner light propels us on our life journey. It holds our sense of self, our confidence, and our ability to love. Without constant introspection, self-observation, and purpose, we tend to let the mundane day-to-day humdrum in our lives obscure our light over time—so much so that at some point it becomes unrecognizable even to us! It is like failing to wash your car regularly. You know what happens to the appearance of your car after regular use on the road. The same thing happens to your inner light.

If you've stayed with me this far, we are almost there. My point is that your inner light is driving you toward a purpose. It's your responsibility as keeper of your light to find that purpose. Happiness is derived from identifying that purpose and making the connections to all the elements of your life. Purpose helps you coordinate each element to focus on a common goal, just as if it were player on a team.

Listen to Yourself

Meditation, prayer, and contemplation are all ways in which you can listen to the voice of your inner light. Take time to appreciate what's going on inside and outside. Most of us are so hurried and busy that we never take time to listen to what truly makes us happy. When we do take time to quiet our minds, we come into contact with what we are really focused on and how we are operating. It's easy just to keep moving and never listen because once you do listen up, you've then got to do something about it. What activities get you to a place where you can listen? For Vernon, it's standing in front of the ocean or sitting on a porch and looking out into nature. Find your place to listen.

Long-term Happiness Should Never Be Sacrificed

Certain adjustments will need to be made throughout your life to allow for your present happiness as well as laying a solid foundation for future happiness. You should never overreact to short-term sacrifices. Watch out for when those sacrifices become long-term and no end is in sight. A few examples of long-term sacrifices to avoid are:

- **A job that consistently makes you miserable**—There are many jobs out there and sometimes you may even need to change careers in order to find happiness and fulfillment. These changes can be dramatic but sometimes they are necessary. The first step toward getting back on track is interviewing. During the course of the interview process, you will either discover a better opportunity or you will realize that your current job is not as bad as you thought and you need to reset your expectations.
- **A relationship that makes you miserable**—Get out of it! Never stay in a relationship that makes you miserable. It is best to identify problems in your relationship early and work through them in a calm and rational manner. Sometimes people are not capable of this; in that case, leave . . . now! It will not get any easier and you are only wasting your time by staying. The longer you stay with the wrong person only decreases the odds of you finding the right person.

Inner Peace Accompanies True Happiness

During the course of writing this book, I observed that the most common trait of the happiest people in my life is that they have inner peace. This inner peace manifests itself in being spiritual and truly tolerant of all people in a nonjudgmental way. This is the level I am working toward, but I am not there yet.

Creating a Structure for Your Happiness Is Important

In order to help you create a structure for understanding and achieving your happiness, I have developed the worksheet on the next page (a user-friendly version is also available at TheSuccessGift. com). This will help you set and achieve your expectations. It will also help you ensure that these expectations are not inhibiting your ability to build a solid foundation for your happiness in the future.

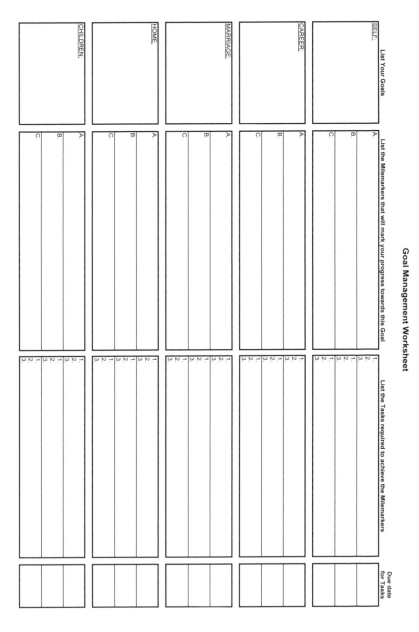

Now that you have a solid understanding of happiness and the underlying structure, it is time to focus on success, both financial and non-financial. The non-financial successes, such as being a great spouse, a caring parent, or an active member of your community, I call achievements.

CHAPTER 13:
FINANCIAL SUCCESS AND ACHIEVEMENTS

We are only on this planet for a finite period, so why not make it worthwhile? As Vernon mentioned in the last chapter, you are the "keeper of the light." It is a light that is full of both potential and purpose. Potential is all that you are capable of doing to fulfill a general purpose in your life and in the world. Without a clear purpose and action, your potential will be wasted. Over the course of our lives, we hone in on our purpose for being here; hopefully we discover it sooner rather than later. You have probably seen some young people who are already clear on their purpose, while some middle-aged folks are still struggling to define it. Vernon was in his mid-forties before he discovered his purpose. Prior to that, it was all about him. Though there are times when you have to be an egoist, most of the time you spend in life will be helping others.

To make success easier to discuss, we'll discuss it in two separate ways: financial success and life achievements. The financial side of success is generally defined as career accomplishments, which are usually quantified by income level. Life achievements are defined as accomplishments in all other areas of your life.

You achieve financial success and life achievements by setting goals for yourself based on what you define as your purpose. This allows you to have more focus and direction. Financial success and life achievements form the milestones along the way to fulfilling your purpose. If your purpose is to travel the world (a literal journey) to help the poor or to spread the faith, your financial success and life achievements would be accomplishments along that journey as you are fulfilling your purpose. Before you set off on this journey, you should create a plan with the short-term being well defined and some objectives for the long-term. This process is called goal setting. The next step is to break down these goals into milestones so that you have a clearly defined path to achieving those goals. Please know that the path is always evolving as you take in more information through your experiences. It's like running toward the horizon. Your direction is clear, but as you move forward, different terrain comes into view that you may not have anticipated. If you have a plan that is fueled by goals and purpose, your next steps will be clearer. Once you've achieved your short-term goals, set new and higher goals.

We now need to clarify the difference between a goal and an expectation (as discussed in previous chapters). There are three main differences:

- Goals are more *dynamic*, whereas expectations tend to be *static* and change less often. Upon achieving goals, new ones should be set that can take you to even greater heights.
- Expectations are met on a regular, usually daily, basis. Accomplishing a goal may take a much longer period of time.
- Accomplishing expectations makes us *happy*, whereas achieving goals makes your life fulfilling.

Remember that our brain has two parts: emotional and logical. The logical part of our brain needs specific expectations so that the emotional side will know how to feel or react.

Many leaders believe that you should inspect what you expect. This practice works well in both your business and your personal life. A boss gives an assignment to someone that reports to him. Every so often, she checks in to see how the project is progressing. A mom asks her son to clean his room before he goes out. You can bet that she will take a peek at that room prior to his exit. Every week or so, you should take a few moments to "inspect" where you are in your goals.

You Are a Custodian of Your Light

The definition of a custodian is a person who looks after and protects something. This is a temporary position, as we will all move on to something different (hopefully better) and we will also eventually retire. All positions are temporary, whether it is as a student, job, friend, spouse, parent, or volunteer. We need to observe and learn from others how they handled these roles and then we must try to find a way to be a little bit better student, worker, friend, spouse, and the like. The final stage is to turn over the responsibilities to the next person so they can also learn from what we did and improve even more upon that. Everyone should:

1. Always be respectful of those ahead of you and learn from them.
2. Improve the situation to the extent you can.
3. Help the next person so that he or she can improve on what you have done.
4. Leave the world a better place than when you came on it.

Plan Your Legacy

The best way to set your goals and keep the big picture in perspective is to plan your funeral. This sounds odd but you need to ask yourself questions such as:

- Who will be at my funeral?
- What will they say about me?
- How will my family feel?
- Will it be a sad occasion or a celebration of the life I led?
- Where will my funeral be?
- Did I make this world a better place?
- What accomplishments am I most proud of?
- How successful was I?
- Is there anything I wish I had done but didn't?

Now it is up to you to decide how you want to be remembered and to make it happen before it is too late.

Enjoy the Journey and Do It the Right Way

The journey is what makes achieving a goal so fulfilling. The struggles, failures, mistakes, growth, learning opportunities, and victories are usually more memorable than the actual point at which you achieve your goal. The journey requires character and integrity. Shortcuts causing you to compromise your morals or ethics will taint the achievement of the goal. This means that, in many cases, how you achieve a goal is more important than the goal itself.

This reminds me of when I was at a Chicago Cubs game many years back. My friends and I had front-row seats right behind the visitors' on-deck circle. It was a beautiful afternoon in late May and the ivy on the outfield wall was just coming into full bloom. It was a perfect day for baseball. To my left was a father and his ten-year-old son. There is nothing more pure than enjoying a baseball game with your son on a beautiful afternoon at Wrigley Field.

The boy had a baseball glove and was prepared to catch a foul ball to commemorate this perfect day. He got so excited every time a ball came close, but no balls had come close enough to catch as of yet. During the course of the game, I got to know the father and son and I learned that the father only wanted to help his son catch a foul ball. Finally, in the eighth inning, there was a lefty at the plate and he chopped a foul ball that took a cherry hop right to the boy. Just before the ball hit the leather, a forty-five-year-old man reached in front of three people, including the dad, and grabbed the ball.

I have rarely seen someone do something so heartless. Everyone asked this person to give the ball to the child and he firmly refused. When it was obvious that this man was unencumbered by common sense and good manners, I decided to taint the ball for the rest of his life by saying, "For the rest of your life when you look at that ball, I want you to remember that you stole it from a child."

You could say that this man achieved his goal of catching a foul ball at a Cubs game, but the way he did it was completely wrong—it is likely that he will not find joy from accomplishing this goal because of the journey he took to achieve it.

There is another factor to consider on your life journey, particularly when it comes to financial success. Are you in it for the power, money, or both? If you want both, do not choose a profession like a politician or a head of a charity. You cannot become wealthy as a politician or working for a charitable organization unless you do something illegal or, at the very least, unethical.

One last point when it comes to the journey. Achieving goals has much more to do with work ethic than it does with the wealth of your parents. Many people want to discount others' success as "being born with a silver spoon in his or her mouth." Admittedly, there is a short period in your twenties that is easier for people whose parents are able to help financially. Shortly thereafter, performance is recognized and it is no longer relevant who your parents are. Don't assume that your parents' success will translate to you, and remember that there are many people who have made great accomplishments with little help from their parents.

Pride comes from achieving goals while doing it the right way.

Financial Success Is Not Everything, But It Sure Is Important

Financial success helps you to first afford the necessities in life and then other modern conveniences. We live in an economic society that requires some level of financial success in order to be happy. This level will vary for each individual person, though, and you must decide where those levels fall.

If you never sacrifice personal time (and thus a portion of your happiness) you will not be financially successful. If you never take the time to enjoy your financial success, you will never be happy.

Financial success and happiness are difficult to balance.

Financial Success Usually Comes before Accomplishing Achievements

The focus of your time in your twenties should primarily be on yourself and your career. As your career leads to financial stability, you can then focus on other areas including family and helping others. Achievements require you to spend time and money. Dedicating too many resources to these efforts too early in your life will limit your potential in the future.

In your early twenties, go ahead and focus on your career. That will enable you to achieve great things for the next fifty or more years of your life.

True Fulfillment Comes from Giving Back and the Achievements We Accomplish

Financial success is often the vehicle and foundation that helps you accomplish your desired achievements. Your goals for achievements can vary from being an inspirational spouse to actively participating in your child's life to helping elderly parents to volunteering to help less fortunate people to achieving spiritual fulfillment. It is accomplishing these types of goals that will enable you to be truly fulfilled and happy. Giving back can be in the form of time and/or money. We need to leave the world a better place than it was when our ancestors left it to us. This is why achievements are ultimately more important than financial success.

Although there are many situations that remind us that there is much more that needs to be done to help the less fortunate, one of the qualities that make this country great is the generosity that we dedicate to those in need.

Giving back is the main ingredient in leading a truly fulfilling life.

With Success Comes Great Responsibility

It is easy to see the benefits of great success, including money, power, influence, status, and the like. At times, successful people forget that there is great responsibility that is bestowed upon them, like it or not. You must use success for good and not selfish reasons. When success becomes purely selfish, negative elements tend to surface like greed, misjudging your intelligence, and overestimating your value to society. When this occurs, there are many people in society who thrive on bringing those types of people back down to reality.

Successful people must lead by example.

Use the Simple Things You Savor as a Reward

When you accomplish a goal, be sure to celebrate. Too often people who achieve a goal set the next one so quickly that they fail to enjoy their success. One of the best ways to celebrate is to experience one of the simple things in life (or to take a great vacation).

Creating a Structure for Your Success Is Essential

Prior to creating a structure for success, you must understand your personal needs. Ask yourself these questions:

- How much money do I want to make?
- Do I want to be married someday? If so, how can I be the best spouse I can be?
- Do I want to own my own home someday? Describe what you would envision it to look.
- Do I want children someday? If so, what role do I want to play in their lives?
- What makes me happy?
- What are my passions?
- How do I want to give back?
- What level of spiritual fulfillment do I want to reach?
- How do I want people to remember me?

As you answer these questions, you will better understand who you are and where your realistic passions lie. Now that you know who you are, you can set your goals appropriately. Use your answers to the questions above to complete the following worksheet that will enable you to create a structure for accomplishing your goals in an efficient manner (a more user-friendly version is available at TheSuccessGift. com). It will also ensure that you are setting reasonable goals that can be readily achieved. The worksheet breaks those goals all the way down to the task level. This will aide you in managing your accomplishments, so you can be headed on the most effective and direct path toward fulfilling your goals. Working hard is not enough; you must also work smartly.

Accomplishing goals is easier when you see regular progress. That is why setting due dates is so important. Your life will never go as planned. By setting due dates, you can ensure you are making planned progress and adjusting your goals as events in your life mandate.

A sense of control over your situation and future are essential.

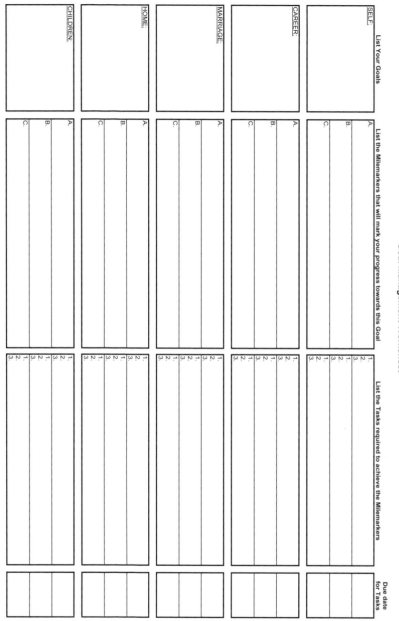

Goal Management Worksheet

List Your Goals | List the Milemarkers that will mark your progress towards this Goal | List the Tasks required to achieve the Milemarkers | Due date for Tasks

SELF:

CAREER:

MARRIAGE:

HOME:

CHILDREN:

This is the last part of the matrix of life addressed in this book. Now it is time to create your masterpiece by building your own matrix of life in the final chapter.

Chapter 14:
Building Your Masterpiece

Over the last thirteen chapters you have learned to apply logic, sequence, and structure to many challenging concepts. You have also learned how to isolate the core elements of your life into specific categories and to understand how these elements influence one another. Now that you can identify these individual elements, it is time to assemble them so you can pursue the goals *you* want. It is time to start building *your* masterpiece.

We discussed earlier in this book *Battle of Waterloo*, the huge painting at the Rijksmuseum in Amsterdam, which the artist painted one panel of a grid at a time. We recommend learning a similar step-by-step way to managing this overwhelming and complex challenge. Your life plan will ultimately form an entire portrait of great depth and complexity, but first you will want to sketch the smaller drafts that combine to make the larger painting. Then, you will need to consider how these components combine to create the larger canvas. As time progresses, you will systematically add color and depth to the painting to gradually fulfill your vision. From time to time, there are details that will change from the sketch. Not only is that acceptable but it is encouraged, because all great plans must allow for some flexibility. There is no way you can anticipate everything at a single point in time.

As you begin to build your masterpiece, remember that the only two mandatory core elements of your life are *self* and *career*. All other core elements are optional. You may be thinking to yourself that you have already committed to another area in addition to self and career. If that's the case, this becomes your core starting point. It is your reality. Either way, in order to include additional elements in your life, it must meet all three of the following requirements:

- You must have the *desire* to have that element be a part of your life.
- You must have the *time* to dedicate to be successful at that new element.
- You must have the *money* to cover the additional expenses of the new element.

These three things make up our decision triangle. If you do not meet all three of the requirements for the optional elements of your life, do not include them. Not meeting all three of these requirements will cause additional stress and lead to unhappiness.

As you advance through your life, please remember that order is important. Each core element lays a solid foundation for the next. You must master each individual element before progressing to the next. You must decide how to handle the additional time and financial constraints that each element presents before you are ready for the next challenge. Each element, when opened, makes life noticeably more complicated and demanding. When you do it right, however, your life will become even more fulfilling. When done wrong, your life will be very difficult and frustrating.

If you decide to commit to a relationship with a partner, it will be important to define your matrix of life as a team. You should combine finances and time management, and you must plan career decisions as a team as well. Any prospective couple should work together on their matrix in preparation for their marriage. This will pinpoint any areas of logistical incompatibility. Couples should explore and understand these differences before making a relationship commitment. Committed relationships and marriages have a dramatically higher success rate when two people love each other *and* when they are logistically compatible.

As you develop your matrix of life, remember that *happiness, financial success,* and *life achievements* add depth to your life. These are often comingled to the point of confusion, so let's review them one more time.

Happiness

Happiness is defined as consistently meeting or exceeding your expectations. The more reasonable your expectations, the more often you will meet those expectations, resulting in a higher level of happiness for you. As a friend of mine once said, "Manage your expectations." You'll see the results—you'll be calmer, more focused, and better able to make good decisions.

Financial Success and Life Achievements

Financial success is defined as the accomplishments in your career, whereas a life achievement refers to accomplishments in all other aspects of your life. Achievements are your personal stamp left on this planet that makes it better than before you were here. To achieve success in these areas, you need to set high goals for yourself. As you achieve those goals, you will set new and higher goals.

Many who set high goals and achieve success also set very high expectations for themselves. When people fail to achieve their expectations consistently, they can become very unhappy. This is why some successful people are not happy. Note that you will need to have clear expectations in the short-term so that your logical or rational side knows what to expect. If you do this, even through tough times where you are doing tasks that you may not enjoy, you can still be happy about the fact that you are on track to achieving long-term success.

To be happy and successful, you must set high, achievable goals along with reasonable expectations.

See the Negative Prior to Pursuing the Positive

Most of the positives in life are accompanied by some negatives. When weighing options, you will make a better decision when the positives outweigh the negatives. The negatives usually include additional expenses and time constraints. They can also include a loss of personal freedom and independence. Always look carefully at the negatives before pursuing the positives. Once comfortable with the negatives, it is time to aggressively pursue the positive.

Easy versus Fulfilling Life

The "easy" definition of life is to have a career, rent an apartment or home, and stay single. Although this will keep stress at the lowest level possible, many people will want to add more core elements in search of more fulfillment. For some, the most "fulfilling" definition of life includes all of the core elements of the matrix of life along with achieving a high level of happiness, financial success, and goals. This "fulfilling" definition can only be achieved when a solid foundation is built for each new core element.

Please know that you do not have to have it all to lead a fulfilling life.

Be Comfortable with Your Choices

From this point forward, you must live your life based on the decisions *you* make. In other words: own your decisions. When you make a decision based on someone else's advice or to please another person, you will still own the consequences. By urging you to live your life based on the decisions *you* make, we emphasize that *you* consider the decisions and what they mean and why you are making them. Whomever you may be trying to please with a decision is not likely to be sharing your pain if the decision works out poorly.

Understand how each decision connects to or affects other decisions you will make in other elements. Your life will differ from the lives of the people around you, even though the elements may be the same.

Life Is Fragile

One of my favorite songs is "Live Like You Were Dying" by Tim McGraw. This song is about his father, baseball legend Tug McGraw, being diagnosed with cancer and how he responded to this horrible news. The wisdom Tug bestowed upon his son is to live life to the fullest, have fun, push your boundaries, be a caring parent, a loving spouse, and a great friend, and to stay connected to your spirituality. You do not have as much time as you think to do everything you want in life. Tug realized that there were certain areas of his life where he was underperforming, and it was only when he found out he had cancer that he realized these areas. He immediately changed in these important areas because he did not want to be remembered in a negative way. Had he lived life like he was dying, he would have been more aware of all aspects of his life at an earlier stage.

As you achieve more in all areas of your life, remember that the happier and more successful you become, the more costly your mistakes also become. This is because you have more to lose. There are no shortcuts!

Building Your Masterpiece

Now it is time to build *your* masterpiece (a more user-friendly version is available at TheSuccessGift.com). You will use the matrix of life as the general gridline structure that will help you organize your aspirations and then apply your sketch of general thoughts to the large canvas of life. This template pulls together all the core elements of life along with managing stress, expectations, and goals into one place. Nothing ever goes exactly according to plan, but if you have a plan, you will accomplish much more and it will be easier to manage any unexpected changes.

As you go through this exercise please keep this in mind: If your aspirations do not work on paper, they certainly won't work in reality. Start from the "top down." This means that you should identify the major factors that are a part of your life. Then go "bottom up" by accumulating all the details to ensure that you are not in conflict or that you are not overcommitting your time, money, or social capabilities. Adjustments will likely be required to your "top down" factors. Keep going "top down" and then "bottom up" until everything is in balance. Ensure that your life also allows for some flexibility and cushion in your valuable resources to accommodate the unexpected changes that will occur throughout your life.

Build YOUR Matrix of Life

	MANDATORY ELEMENTS		_OPTIONAL ELEMENTS_			
	Self	Career	Marriage	Home	Children	Pets
Desire: Do you want this core element of life? - At what age? - Why or why not? What are the positives of this element? What are the negatives that must be considered?	YES Mandatory	YES Mandatory				
Time: Do you have the time for this element? - How much time will you dedicate? - What sacrifices will you make to allow time for optional elements?	YES	YES				
Money: Can you afford this element? - How much will it cost? - What sacrifices will you make to afford optional elements?	YES	YES				
Happiness What makes you happy? What are your expectations?						
Financial Success and Achievements How successful do you want to be in your career? What achievements do you want to accomplish in your life? What are your significant goals?						

Enjoy!

Enjoy *your* life as you define it. Do not view this process as a onetime event. Continually revisit this exercise, particularly in times of change or unhappiness, to ensure you are on track toward creating your masterpiece. Also, avoid living your life by others' standards, opinions, or material possessions. Everyone is different and satisfaction must come from within.

A balanced and optimistic approach to life is the key. No matter how well you plan, bad things *will* happen. Take problems in stride and they will be put behind you. You will also want to streamline your life as you get busier. Consistently work to improve your ability to manage stress resulting from your time, finances, and social capabilities. Eliminate distractions that occupy your time but that do not put you any closer to achieving your matrix of life.

Now it is up to you to live a fulfilling life by constantly developing and perfecting *your* masterpiece. Make it happen!

AFTERWORD:
SEMINARS—"MOTIVE-ACTION-AL"

One of the most exciting outcomes of writing this book is being able to partner with a passionate motivator like Vernon Roberts. I have never witnessed a better professional speaker and coach (visit evokelearning.com to see what I'm talking about). Together, we are excited to offer a variety of seminars and webinars based on demand from this book. Our offerings are constantly updated at TheSuccessGift.com.

Here is our **warning** to you: If you want to experience success without putting in some amount of work, do not come to our seminars. Our seminars are not like those infomercial "lose weight without exercise" plans or "get abs by wearing this special belt" offers. Our workshops provide you with the motivation and the tools to create structure around your life decisions. Many workshops that are available in this vein are generally ineffective for two reasons: they are either simply motivational without any defined process, or they are only a forum to complain about what is going wrong at work and at home. We know that motivation fades when you have to put out that first fire the next day. You can look on your shelf or credenza and find the materials from that last motivational workshop that you took where the materials are now under a pile or covered with dust. The goal of our workshop is to be not only motivational but MOTIVE-ACTION-AL! In other words, you must be motivated to act. When you leave one of our workshops you'll have two choices. The first choice is to do nothing. Some of you will take this option. The second choice is to use our easy tools to kick-start a more compelling and fulfilling life. We think it's an obvious choice and, by the way, it's your first test.

If you are a manager or business owner, you have probably noticed that there has been no way for a company to help employees improve their personal lives other than offering underutilized Employee Assistance Programs. With us, it's a win-win situation. Employees benefit from our course because they learn how to structure work and home life for greater fulfillment and efficiency, and the company benefits because employees do not bring as many distracting problems to work. Vernon and I have developed a unique workshop that can be tailored to the specific needs of your company where employees, particularly those who have recently graduated, will understand the importance of proper structure in their lives. This proper structure will help them not only be more effective at work but also lead more fulfilling lives outside of work. It is obvious that an employee who has proper structure in their private life will be more effective at work. Additionally, our seminar leverages the financial expertise of both me and Vernon to help employees understand that there is nothing more important at work than profitability. We are able to break down profitability in a unique way that helps every single employee understand their important role in maximizing profitability. This is why this is also the only work-life balance seminar that can be evaluated in terms of the cost justification method "payback period." In virtually every case it has been less than a month!

We are also in the process of offering a seminar and webinar for individuals who are preparing for the real world. This is essential for anyone who wants to get a jump on their competition when they get into the working world. A quick start out of the gates is essential to long-term success and happiness. Visit TheSuccessGift.com for details on the webinars available and when the seminar will be making a stop in a city near you.

ABOUT THE AUTHORS

 CHIP SAWICKI attended Wake Forest University in Winston-Salem, North Carolina, majoring in accounting. Upon graduation, Chip returned to his home state of New Jersey to work for Price Waterhouse, where he earned his license as a Certified Public Accountant.

Chip moved to Dallas, Texas, to serve on the Exxon engagement, where one of his clients was the Dallas Stars. Upon developing an expertise in accounting and finance, along with his professional sports experience, the Texas Rangers offered Chip the opportunity to be Controller. After making financial operations much better, in 1998 Chip was promoted to Vice President, Finance for Southwest Sports Group for the Rangers and the Stars, where he held the Chief Financial Officer role for both teams.

As a result of a shift in responsibilities at the highest levels of Southwest Sports Group, Chip was replaced and forced to start a new phase of his career. At this time, Chip decided to make a complete career change, working in business development for Jefferson Wells International.

After several successful years there, Chip decided to take a major risk. He and an associate started Total Home Solutions, a hassle-free solution to home maintenance. Although it was a great idea and a tremendous team was built, the company started to run low on capital and they decided to close it down.

Shortly after, Chip's wife was presented with an outstanding career opportunity that required the family to relocate to Charlotte, North Carolina. During this process, Chip decided to be a stay-at-home Dad. It was during the time, while his two sons were in school, that Chip wrote and refined this book.

After helping his children get settled in school and his wife in a new job, Chip began teaching Introduction to Financial Accounting to sophomores at his alma matter, Wake Forest University. Additionally, he holds leadership roles in his community.

And that brings us to today . . .

VERNON ROBERTS is a leadership facilitator, coach, and performance consultant. Vernon works with individuals, teams and organizations to increase effectiveness, After almost twenty years in financial services, he founded of Evoke Learning & Performance, a provider of custom corporate education. Vernon has four children and he and his wife live in Mathews, North Carolina.